SCHOLASTIC

ACTIVE™

Grammar

Practice Book 5

Rosemary Allen

Name ______________________________

Class ______________________________

Previously published as Grammar Skills 5 by Learners Publishing Pte Ltd.

First edition 2012
Reprinted 2012, 2013, 2014 (thrice), 2015 (twice), 2016, 2017 (twice), 2019, 2021, 2022, 2023 2024

ISBN 978-81-8477-750-5

CONTENTS

 ISBN 978-81-8477-750-5

To Teachers and Parents

The study of English grammar in schools is changing as educators become increasingly aware of the important role context plays in language learning. The functional use of grammar has become a feature of English syllabuses around the world.

Active Grammar Practice Books have been written specifically to provide students with valuable links between basic, traditional grammatical concepts and the functional contexts in which they are used. The activities represent a blend of traditional and functional approaches to describe how texts 'work' in real-life situations and why certain grammatical choices are considered appropriate. Traditional grammar serves to provide students with the special terminology needed to talk about grammar, while functional grammar is intended to improve communicative competence by showing students how grammar works in the context of different text types.

The exercises in this book give students systematic guidance in developing an understanding of grammatical concepts. Throughout the books there are panel notes that give hints for correct usage and highlight exceptions to grammar rules, as well as provide simple non-technical definitions to help students understand the exercises. Many of the exercises incorporate learner-centred activities that include completing rhymes and short stories, solving riddles and puzzles, doing word searches and seeing 'language-in-action'. At the same time, the activities provide teachers with a range of techniques to use, techniques that have proven highly successful with both native and non-native speakers of English. The exercises are graded, but include challenging ones to motivate as well as interest the students.

It is hoped that teachers will find this series a valuable tool in their teaching programme, one that will provide young learners with a fascinating journey into the world of English language and a sound knowledge of how it works.

 ISBN 978-81-8477-750-5

1 Abstract and Collective Nouns

Grammar Help

Concrete nouns are things you can touch and see, like ***pen*** and ***pencil.*** **Abstract nouns** are ideas or concepts. They are things you can't see or touch, like ***envy*** and ***fear***.

A ***Read the letter below. Fill in the blanks with suitable abstract nouns from the box.***

kindness	joy	relief	gratitude	hope	despair

20 June 2014

Dear Mr Brown,

Please accept my (1) ______________ for the help you gave me yesterday when I was lost. Your (2) ______________ in helping me was certainly appreciated. I had started to lose all (3) ______________ of locating my parents until you came along. What a (4) ______________ it was to hear your friendly voice. You can imagine my (5) ______________ when I realized I was alone in a strange city and my (6) ______________ when you found my mother and father for me.

Your grateful new friend,

Peter

 ISBN 978-81-8477-750-5

B ***Use the abstract nouns in the box to help you complete the sentences. You may need to add other words too.***

hatred	**wickedness**	**danger**	**truth**	**beauty**

1. It is wrong to tell a lie. You should always ______________.
2. Run away quickly. You are ______________.
3. In fairy tales, the stepmothers usually get punished ______________ ______________.
4. Enemy countries let ______________ lead to war.
5. Fashion models are chosen ______________.

Grammar Help

Some nouns are made by adding a suffix to a verb, an adjective or even another noun; for example: *happiness, jealousy, puzzlement, friendship* and *appearance.*

C ***Look at the three words in each box. Write a suffix you could add to make each of the words into an abstract noun. Then list the nouns you have made on the lines provided. The first one is done for you.***

1. happy kind lonely + **ness**

   happiness ______ kindness ______ loneliness ______

2. enjoy agree punish + ______

   ______ ______ ______

3. discover honest injure + ______

   ______ ______ ______

4. create act introduce + ______

   ______ ______ ______

 ISBN 978-81-8477-750-5

D ***Change the words in brackets into nouns to complete the sentences.***

The boy could not understand (1) ______________ (multiply) and (2) ______________ (divide) in spite of his teacher's (3) ______________ (explain) and extra (4) ______________ (instruct) after school. It was not because of (5) ______________ (lazy). He wanted his teacher's (6) ______________ (approve) and he always completed his (7) ______________ (correct), but he seemed to lack the (8) ______________ (confident) to find the (9) ______________ (solve).

Grammar Help

A **collective noun** is the special name that is given to a number of things, animals or people that are grouped together and spoken of as one whole; for example, *an army of soldiers.*

E ***Name some groups that you could find in the locations below. You may use the collective nouns in the box to help you.***

tribe	**string**	**troupe**	**bench**	**pride**	**congregation**
band	**pod**	**horde**	**comb**	**set**	

1. On a stage: ______________
2. In a church: ______________
3. In a courthouse: ______________
4. In Africa: ______________
5. In a jewellery box: ______________
6. In the ocean: ______________
7. In a kitchen: ______________

 ISBN 978-81-8477-750-5

Grammar Help

Usually you think of collective nouns as a single body, so you use a singular verb with them. For example: *The* ***army*** *of soldiers* ***looks*** *very impressive.*

However, when you think of the group *as individuals* you use a plural verb with that collective noun.

F ***Underline the more appropriate verb for each sentence.***

1. The company of actors (was/were) happy to perform for the Queen.
2. A string of pearls (do/does) not cost as much as a diamond ring.
3. The jury (is/are) made up of twelve people.
4. The jury (is/are) still making up their minds.
5. The symphony orchestra (is/are) playing here next week.
6. The orchestra (is/are) still tuning up their instruments.
7. Our team (is/are) wearing their new shoes.
8. Our team (is/are) the best in school.
9. The office staff (is/are) enjoying the outing.
10. The crowd of spectators (rush/rushes) forward as each celebrity arrives.

 ISBN 978-81-8477-750-5

2 Pronouns

Grammar Help

Personal pronouns take the place of nouns. They can be the subject or object of the sentence.

The pronouns **I, you, he, she, it, we, they** are used in the subject position. The pronouns **me, you, him, her, it, us, them** are used in the object position.

Writers often use first person and second person pronouns to express opinions. This makes readers feel as though the writer is addressing them personally. This technique is used a lot in the writing of expositions.

A ***Fill in the blanks in this short expositon. You need to use suitable pronouns in the first and second person (I, me, we, us, you), as well as reflexives (myself, ourselves, yourself, yourselves).***

Many people today lead inactive lives. How do (1) ________________ prefer to spend your leisure time? Are (2) ________________ a lazy couch potato, too? If so, (3) ________________ may want to seriously reconsider your lifestyle.

My friends and (4) ________________ used to be like that, but we have changed. These days, (5) ________________ are not the kind of students who sit in front of a television set or a computer for hours on end. In fact, our parents actively encourage (6) ________________ to get outside and explore the outdoors—to exercise and breathe fresh air. As for (7) ________________, I have learnt to balance my study with leisure activities. Since then, my examination marks have improved amazingly and (8) ________________ feel so much more energetic. My parents are very proud of (9) ________________ but, best of all, I feel proud of (10) ________________.

 ISBN 978-81-8477-750-5

Grammar Help

- ***Possessive pronouns*** talk about things belonging to people or animals. They are: ***mine, yours, his, hers, its, theirs*** and ***ours.***
- **Indefinite pronouns** do not stand for any particular person, place or thing, for example: ***anyone, someone.***
- **Demonstrative pronouns** point out which one/ones you are talking about. They are ***this, that, these*** and ***those.***
- **Reciprocal pronouns** tell you that each person in a group is doing the same thing to the other person or persons, for example: ***each other, one another.***

B ***Read each sentence and identify the pronoun in bold print. Write the type of pronoun on the line after the sentence. The first one is done for you.***

1. **They** are going to the cinema tomorrow. Personal pronoun
2. The pink towel is not **mine.** ____________
3. **Anyone** over ten years of age can join the club. ____________
4. **Those** are my books. ____________
5. These smelly socks must be **his.** ____________
6. Can **somebody** help me with this heavy bag? ____________
7. The police officer warned **us** not to leave our bicycles unlocked. ____________
8. They congratulated **each other** on winning the doubles in the tennis tournament. ____________
9. Why are you afraid of **them**? ____________
10. You can't take **that:** it is **mine.** ____________

 ISBN 978-81-8477-750-5

C ***Here are a few scenarios. What might the person say? Use a suitable pronoun (or more) in your answer. Underline the pronouns you used. The first one is done as an example.***

1. Michelangelo is feeling proud. He has just finished painting the ceiling of the Sistine Chapel and expects the work to last for centuries.

   Michelangelo: <u>This</u> is my masterpiece! <u>It</u> will last for centuries.

   <u>Everyone</u> will admire <u>it</u>.

2. Mary is angry. Her five-year-old brother has taken Mother's lipstick and drawn pictures over her maths homework.

   Mary: ____

   ____

3. Father is overseas. He is showing photographs of the family to some relatives who live there, and telling them about the people in the pictures.

   Father: _______________________________________

   ____

4. Benjamin is feeling thirsty. He is paraplegic and goes around in a wheelchair. He is also very independent.

   Ben: ____

   ____

5. Miss Lee is anxious. The school inspectors are coming and the class has been misbehaving.

   Miss Lee: ______________________________________

   ____

 ISBN 978-81-8477-750-5

D ***Fill in each blank with a suitable pronoun. Then write the type of pronoun you have used in the sentence. The first one is done for you.***

1. Mum, have ____you____ seen my red cap? ____personal pronoun (subject)____

2. You wrote the address down in that notebook, but is the notebook ____________? ____________

3. I think there's ____________ at the door. ____________

4. Why can't the two of you help ____________ instead of fighting? ____________

5. Hello! Who is ____________ speaking, please? ____________

6. Have ____________ left the building? ____________

7. The book is ____________ because it has my initials on it. ____________

8. Come here! Which of ____________ are your books? ____________

9. ____________ will get to the station themselves. ____________

10. Pass ____________ a ruler, please. I dare not move from here. ____________

 ISBN 978-81-8477-750-5

3 Reflexive and Interrogative Pronouns

Grammar Help

Reflexive pronouns are those that end in ***-self*** or ***-selves.*** They are: **myself, yourself, himself, herself, itself, ourselves, themselves** and **yourselves.**

- A reflexive pronoun refers to the subject of the sentence.
- A reflexive pronoun may be used for emphasis, for example: *The principal himself congratulated me for my excellent project work.*

A ***Add a reflexive pronoun to each of the following sentences.***

1. The greedy boy served ____________________ before anyone else.
2. You can't blame ____________________ for other people's mistakes.
3. The injured dog dragged ____________________ home.
4. I told ____________________ I would do better next time.
5. She kept all of the chocolates for ____________________.
6. Paul went to the mirror and looked closely at ____________________.
7. They were told to clean up the place ____________________ and not to leave a mess.
8. Mr and Mrs Lang booked the tickets for ____________________, but not for us.
9. The independent little girl wanted to dress ____________________ without any help.
10. The villagers mended the wooden bridge by ____________________.

 ISBN 978-81-8477-750-5

11. The car seemed to move off down the driveway by ____________________.

12. The triumphant team treated ____________________ to a victory party.

B ***Complete the sentences using reflexive pronouns to show emphasis.***

1. When we looked over our notes, we ____________________ couldn't understand what we had written.

2. You ____________________ told me about the incident over the telephone; that was how I knew you were involved.

3. I ____________________ recommended that we should go by train, but now I'm sorry I suggested it.

4. The residents managed to put out the fire ____________________. The fire engines were delayed by a traffic accident along the way.

5. The cashier was inefficient and untruthful; she ____________________ had made the mistake that she blamed me for.

6. The king ____________________ rewarded the knight with a bag of gold; he had rescued the princess from a gang of outlaws.

7. The dog swam out to save the little boy struggling in the river, but the dog ____________________ was carried away by the strong current.

8. The teacher told her class, "The test was a simple one, but all of you have failed it. Only you ____________________ know why you haven't passed. Please tell me one by one."

 ISBN 978-81-8477-750-5

Grammar Help

Interrogative pronouns are used to ask questions. They are ***who, whose, what*** and ***which***.

- **Who** is usually used as the subject of the verb.
  Whom is only used as the object.
- To find out whether to use **who** or **whom**, try this simple test.
  Replace **who** or **whom** with **he/she** or **him/her**.
  If **he** or **she** sounds right, use **who**.
  If **him** or **her** sounds right, use **whom**.
  For example: *You give something to him not to he, so the question is "To whom did you give it?"*

C ***Form questions to which these statements are answers. Start with the given interrogative pronouns.***

1. The Nile is the longest river in the world.

   Which is the longest river in the world?

2. Those are David's torn trousers over there.

   Whose ________________________________

3. Paul's dirty shoes must have made those marks on the floor.

   What ________________________________

   ____

4. The girl sitting over there is Jane's best friend.

   Who ________________________________

5. I want to study engineering when I go to university.

   What ________________________________

 ISBN 978-81-8477-750-5

6. The film about the grey wolf is my favourite.

   Which ____

7. My father supports Manchester United in the English Premier League.

   Whom ____

D ***Fill in the blanks in the following conversation with* who *or* whom *correctly.***

John: My mother wants me to go for dancing lessons with Jane.

Jack: With (1) ______________?

John: Jane. You know, the girl (2) ______________ lives next door.

Jack: (3) ______________ is going to teach you ballroom dancing?

John: The lady (4) ______________ taught my mum and dad to dance.

Jack: Do you know that Jane's the girl to (5) ______________ I gave the chocolates?

John: So it was you (6) ______________ gave them to her. She didn't know (7) ______________ it was.

Jack: I think I'll join the dance class, too. To (8) ______________ should I apply?

 ISBN 978-81-8477-750-5

4 Relative Pronouns

Grammar Help

Relative pronouns describe the person, animal, thing or place already referred to. They are ***who, whom, whose, which*** and ***that***.

- The relative pronouns **who, whom** and **whose** are used for people, while **which** and **that** are mostly used for animals, places and things.
- **Who** can be used with both the subject and the object of a verb, but **whom** can only be used with the object.
- The relative pronoun **whose** can refer to people, animals or things.

A ***Complete each sentence using the most appropriate of the relative pronouns who, whose, whom, which and that.***

1. The teacher would like the boy ________________ threw the eraser to stand up.
2. The car crashed into a vehicle ________________ was approaching very fast from the opposite direction.
3. I know an old man ________________ can play the guitar very well.
4. This is the shop ________________ sells the CD ________________ you are looking for.
5. The police have arrested the man ________________ is suspected of murder.
6. She is the author ________________ I have heard so much about.
7. I have an aunt ________________ cat is so fat that it cannot sit up properly.
8. We bought a big bag of plums ________________ were not ripe.
9. May's brother plays in the soccer team ________________ has won this year's match again.
10. The bus ________________ leaves at 4:00 pm is the one ________________ goes directly to the library.
11. The teacher was angry with the boy ________________ threw stones at the dog ________________ had been barking at him.
12. The taxi driver, ________________ vehicle hit the kerb, was not hurt.

 ISBN 978-81-8477-750-5

B *Complete each of the sentences with the most likely clause from the box.*

whose mother often works late	whose branches were thick and leafy
whose hands were covered in flour	whose sister is in our netball team
whose parents were very rich	whose book won a national award
whose father is a good pianist	whose face was recognized by witnesses
whose shirt was torn	whose father often buys her books

1. The woman ______________________________
had been baking for the party.

2. The boy ______________________________
had been climbing trees.

3. The children ______________________________
had a lot of expensive toys.

4. The girl ______________________________
takes good care of herself and her younger brother.

5. The girl ______________________________
loves reading and is good at it.

6. The man ______________________________
has been captured by the police.

7. The author ______________________________
is now writing another book for children.

8. The tree, ______________________________,
stood in the field for many years.

9. Tom, ______________________________,
is a very good musician too.

10. Sally, ______________________________,
doesn't like sport at all.

 ISBN 978-81-8477-750-5

C ***Complete each sentence using a clause beginning with the relative pronoun who to give more information about the subject. The first one is done for you. Notice that the relative pronoun is usually followed by a verb.***

1. People __who make fun of others__ do not have many friends.
2. The boy ____________________
was awarded a merit certificate.
3. Mrs Jones, ____________________,
showed me how to sew.
4. Jane, ____________________,
lives next door to my house.
5. Roger, ____________________,
was very kind to me when I first arrived at this school.
6. My uncle, ____________________,
walks with me to the bus stop every morning.
7. The boy, ____________________,
no longer goes to my school.
8. The famous scientist, ____________________,
has won many awards for his work on blood diseases.
9. All the children, ____________________
were allowed to go home early.
10. Those workers ____________________
finally completed the job yesterday.

 ISBN 978-81-8477-750-5

D ***Use the relative pronouns whom, who, which or that to give more information about the objects of these sentences.***

1. The policeman questioned the man ______________________________

____

2. Janet immediately liked the new girl ______________________________

____

3. My friend told me about his teacher ______________________________

____

4. The crew disliked the captain ______________________________

____

5. Alice chose an expensive watch ______________________________

____

6. You can catch the bus ______________________________

____

7. The search party found the little boy ______________________________

____

8. The mother bear cried pitifully for her cub ______________________________

____

9. The farmer trapped the rabbit ______________________________

____

10. She put on the red dress ______________________________

____

 ISBN 978-81-8477-750-5

5 Adjectives: Position, Types and Formation

Grammar Help

Adjectives are words that describe nouns. They are mostly placed before the nouns they describe, but they can be placed after verbs, such as forms of "to be", as well as ***seem***, ***look***, ***appear***.

A ***Write two suitable adjectives to describe the nouns in bold. Notice that the adjectives you are writing come after the nouns they are describing.***

1. The **weather** in winter is ______ ______
2. **Dogs** are extremely ______ ______
3. The **buses** in the morning can be ______ ______
4. **Friends** are always ______ ______
5. **Grammar** is ______ ______
6. Most **people in Singapore** are ______ ______
7. In the evening, the **sun** looks ______ ______
8. **Durians** smell ______ ______

B ***Write two sentences for each adjective below. In the first sentence, use the adjective before the noun. In the second sentence, use the adjective after a suitable verb. An example has been done for you.***

1. rough

(a) The rough stones on the shore hurt her feet.

(b) The stones look rough and they might hurt my feet.

 ISBN 978-81-8477-750-5

2. graceful

(a) ______________________________

(b) ______________________________

3. comfortable

(a) ______________________________

(b) ______________________________

4. dirty

(a) ______________________________

(b) ______________________________

5. sharp

(a) ______________________________

(b) ______________________________

6. cowardly

(a) ______________________________

(b) ______________________________

7. safe

(a) ______________________________

(b) ______________________________

8. familiar

(a) ______________________________

(b) ______________________________

 ISBN 978-81-8477-750-5

Grammar Help

There are many different kinds of adjectives. They can tell you about the **size** (*huge*), **age** (*ancient*), **shape** (*square*), **colour** (*red*), **quality** (*clever*), **origin**—where it comes from (Australian), and **class**—type or group it belongs to (*steel*).

C ***Underline the adjective in each phrase. Decide which type of adjective it is; then write the phrase under the correct heading in the table below.***

a Japanese car — a wooden puppet — an English pound

a short skirt — a plastic bucket — the Singaporean flag

a tall building — a foolish act — a narrow passage

a dangerous road — a shopping mall — a cruel king

a public facility — a thick encyclopaedia — an irate teacher

a Scottish kilt — a large area — a generous act

Size	Quality	Place of Origin	Classification

 ISBN 978-81-8477-750-5

Grammar Help

We generally follow a certain order when using a list of adjectives before a noun.

- The order is: size, age, shape, colour, class, origin; but compound nouns, such as **frying pan** or **horror film**, are not separated. For example: *He held a* ***big, square, red, plastic*** *bucket and* ***battered, black, tin frying*** *pan in his* ***huge, brown*** *hands.*
- Adjectives expressing your own opinion (adjectives of quality) usually come before all other adjectives. The more general adjective (relating to size, etc) is usually put first. For example: *The girl had* ***beautiful, long, black*** *hair.*
- Notice how commas are used to separate the adjectives.

D ***Add adjectives from the brackets to the underlined nouns. Be sure you use them in the correct order. Remember to put in commas between the adjectives.***

1. The lion crouched in the grass. (dry huge long old yellow)

____

____

2. Nothing tastes better than biscuits. (buttery chocolate homemade warm)

____

____

3. The cat sniffed around the tree. (black giant inquisitive oak tiny)

____

____

4. Mrs Brown gave John a calculator. (black Japanese new useful)

____

____

 ISBN 978-81-8477-750-5

5. The <u>boat</u> tossed about on the <u>sea</u>. (ancient angry small vast wooden)

____

____

6. Mrs Taylor placed the <u>clock</u> on the <u>table</u>. (antique brown elegant French wooden)

____

____

Grammar Help

You can change nouns and verbs into adjectives by adding suffixes like **-less**, **-ful**, **-ish**, **-ous**, **-ing**, **-y**, **-able**, **-ive**, **-en**, **-ed**, **-al**, **-ic**, **-ly** and **-ible**.

E ***Complete the rhyme by adding an adjective that has a suffix. The word in bold will help you.***

1. A girl with a **smile** has a ______________ face.
2. A town in the **mountains** is a ______________ place.
3. A doctor of **medicine** is a ______________ man.
4. A plan you can't **use** is a ______________ plan.
5. A car full of **rust** is a ______________ machine.
6. People go to the **tropics** for a ______________ scene.
7. Please **boil** the water; I'd like ______________ eggs for breakfast.
8. Don't think only of your**self**—don't be ______________ to me.
9. A face full of **sorrow** is a ______________ sight.
10. And I'll always **remember** that ______________ night.

 ISBN 978-81-8477-750-5

F ***Use the suffixes in the box to change the following nouns into adjectives.***

-ish	-ous	-ing	-y	-able
-ive	-ic	-ly	-ed	-en

1. How many different adjectives can you make with each noun?

   (a) expense: ______________________

   (b) scene: ______________________

   (c) comfort: ______________________

   (d) friend : ______________________

   (e) wood: ______________________

   (f) care: ______________________

   (g) poison: ______________________

   (h) storm: ______________________

   (i) fool: ______________________

   (j) bore: ______________________

2. Use some of the adjectives you made above to help you fill in this crossword puzzle.

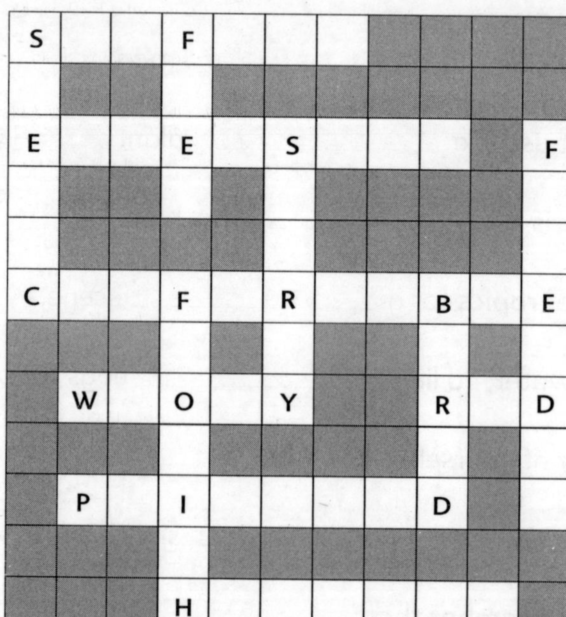

 ISBN 978-81-8477-750-5

3. Here are the clues for the four other adjectives in the crossword.

   (a) "The ____________ Giant" is a story by Oscar Wilde.

   (b) The shop has a ____________ gift-wrapping service.

   (c) My favourite colour is ____________ .

   (d) Peter is very ____________ : he makes the beds and sweeps the floor for his mother.

 ISBN 978-81-8477-750-5

6 Adjectives of Quantity and Comparison

Grammar Help

Adjectives can tell us more about the **amount** or **quantity** of a noun.

- Ordinal numbers (**first, second, third**) are adjectives, too.
- Adjectives showing an indefinite number, such as **few, several, many, some,** are sometimes called **determiners.**
- Adjectives of quantity come before all other adjectives (including adjectives of quality).

A ***Read the rhyme.***

1. Circle the number adjectives and underline the ordinary adjectives.

Lazy Days

One lonely stray dog yapping to be fed,
Two squawking seagulls flying overhead,
Three long-haired buskers playing as a band,
Some happy picnickers resting on the sand

Several tiny rock crabs waiting for the tide
Eight graceful anemones with petals opened wide—
These are some of the things I see at the seaside.

2. Write two lines of your own. Remember to include some adjectives of quantity.

___

___

B ***Use adjectives of definite quantity to complete these sentences. Write the words that fit, not the numerals.***

1. A baker's dozen refers to ____________________ buns.
2. There are ____________________ playing cards in a pack.
3. An octave on the piano refers to ____________________ notes.
4. Quintuplets are ____________________ babies born together to the same mother.
5. A dodecahedron has ____________________ faces.
6. When Abraham Lincoln said "four score years and ten years ago" in 1863, he was talking about something that happened ____________________ years earlier.

Grammar Help

To compare two things, you can use a **comparative** adjective, like **sweeter**. To compare more than two things, you can use a **superlative** adjective, like **sweetest**.

- Comparatives often end in **-er**, while superlatives often end in **-est**.
- The words **more** or **most** are usually placed in front of adjectives that have more than two syllables to make a comparison.

C ***Look at the clothing items on the next page. Write a sentence that answers the questions about them. The first one is done for you.***

1. Which shoes have the highest heels?

   The black court shoes have the highest heels.

2. Which dress is more elegant?

   ____

 ISBN 978-81-8477-750-5

3. Which coat is the longest?

____

4. Which dress is less expensive?

____

5. Which pair of shoes is the least expensive?

____

6. Which coat is the plainest?

____

7. Which shoes are the most comfortable?

____

 ISBN 978-81-8477-750-5

D ***Read these descriptions and write some sentences comparing the information. Remember to use comparatives and superlatives. A sample is done for you.***

Tom King was born in India in 1942. He writes mostly about serious issues. His stories always include a lesson of some kind, and critics say his books are popular because he seems to understand children's problems.

Tom King is a very athletic man who likes to play many sports in his spare time. He also plays the piano and sings in the church choir. On Sundays, he attends church and spends time with his family. Mr King left school at 14 years of age and admits that he has never had much use for formal education.

Sam Prince was born in Australia in 1982. Although mainly a writer of adult books, he enjoys writing humorous books for children. His stories always include jokes and fun activities. Critics say his books are popular because he sees the funny side of life, despite being wheelchair-bound since a horse riding accident five years ago. Although he enjoys listening to music, Mr Prince admits that he is not very musically talented.

A great believer in education, he is currently completing PhD studies.

Jim Lord is a cartoonist who was born in Singapore in 1960. The children's comics he produces feature adventures and excitement. Some critics say his comics are violent and unsuitable for children. However, the comics sell better than any other books or magazines.

In his spare time, Mr Lord likes to travel to exotic places where he says he gains inspiration for his comics. He has no time for music, preferring instead to watch kung fu movies. This appears odd for someone who is highly educated with a PhD in philosophy.

1. Tom King is the least educated of the three writers.
2. __________
3. __________
4. __________
5. __________
6. __________
7. __________

 ISBN 978-81-8477-750-5

Grammar Help

When you compare one thing to two others separately as though they are comparatives, you use the comparative form, or **more**. For example: *A dog is* ***more affectionate*** *than a cat or a guinea pig.* The word **or** is used when three items are being compared in a comparative way.

E ***Compare the subjects given in each tinted box and write a sentence about them using suitable adjectives from the box. Follow the samples given.***

interesting	**important**	**fragrant**	**skilful**
expensive	**dangerous**	**nervous**	**spectacular**

1. A rose is more fragrant than an orchid.
   - rose
   - orchid

2. Lion taming is the most spectacular of the three acts. OR
   Lion taming is more spectacular than juggling or the trapeze.
   - juggling
   - lion taming
   - the trapeze

3. ______________________________
   - mountain climbing
   - parachuting
   - hunting

4. ______________________________
   - cleaning your teeth
   - brushing your hair
   - exercising

5. ______________________________
   - The dentist
   - A savage dog

 ISBN 978-81-8477-750-5

6. ____

____

____

- football players
- pianists
- sculptors

7. ____

____

____

- Books about stamps
- Books about history
- Books about explorers

8. ____

____

____

- A bicycle
- A skipping rope

Grammar Help

Some comparatives are very tricky. Here are some of the tricky irregular forms:

- good, better, best.
- bad, worse, worst
- little, less, least
- many/much, more, most
- far, farther (further), farthest (furthest)
- old, elder, eldest (for people only)

F ***Put the correct form of the tricky comparative given in brackets into the blanks.***

1. Although I'm ________________ at reading and ________________ at maths, my ________________ subject of all is music. (good)

2. This has to be the ________________ week in my life. Monday was a ________________ day as I was late for school; it got ________________ on Tuesday and has not improved since then. (bad)

 ISBN 978-81-8477-750-5

3. I live ________________ from school than Tom, but that is not as ________________ as Jane, who lives quite the ________________ of all. (far)

4. While ________________ in the class play table tennis, ________________ prefer tennis and the ________________ prefer badminton. (many)

5. I have ________________ sympathy for tattletales but I think liars deserve the ________________ respect, even ________________ than bullies. (little)

6. You should listen to me as I am ________________, but neither of us is as ________________ as Dad, since he is the ________________ in the family. (old)

 ISBN 978-81-8477-750-5

7 Adverbials of Manner and Place

Grammar Help

Adverbs add information to verbs, adjectives and other words. They tell you more about the verb, adjective or adverb. Adverbs answer questions about **how** (manner), **where** (place) and **when** (time) an action takes place. They also tell **how often** (frequency) or **how long** (duration) someone does something.

A ***Read the rhyme and underline the adverbs that tell how something is done.***

Snail Watching

Slowly, silently, moves the snail
Carelessly leaving a silver trail.
Resting briefly along the way,
A very small distance takes her nearly a day.

Painfully over sharp rocks she ambles,
Beneath shady ferns and prickly brambles.
Slowly, but surely she crosses a flower
And disappears under a leafy-green bower.

 ISBN 978-81-8477-750-5

B ***The verbs on the bubbles are more expressive words to use for the verb said.***

1. Match each verb in the bubble to an adverb on the right to give more information about the verb. The first one is done for you.

	Verb	Adverb
(a)	announced	• proudly
(b)	sobbed	• curiously
(c)	repeated	• endlessly
(d)	boasted	• nervously
(e)	moaned	• confidently
(f)	enquired	• painfully
(g)	stammered	• hysterically
(h)	warned	• helpfully

 ISBN 978-81-8477-750-5

2. Use the verbs and adverbs to write sentences like the one below. You need to include direct speech.

(a) "I'm going to win the best athlete award this year," Peter announced confidently.

(b) ______

(c) ______

(d) ______

(e) ______

(f) ______

(g) ______

(h) ______

 ISBN 978-81-8477-750-5

Grammar Help

Like adverbs of manner, **adverbial phrases of manner** tell "how". These phrases often include prepositions.

In a sentence, adverbial phrases of manner usually follow a verb or the object. However, they can be used at the beginning of a sentence, to give it some variety.

C ***Make sentences using the adverbial phrases given.***

1. Through hard work, ______________________________

2. ______________________________
in a suspicious manner.

3. Without a care in the world, ______________________________

4. ______________________________
by means of a screwdriver.

5. Without thinking, ______________________________

6. ______________________________
through his carelessness.

7. By rising earlier, ______________________________

8. ______________________________
by train.

9. Without his computer, ______________________________

10. ______________________________
with care.

 ISBN 978-81-8477-750-5

D ***Read this short passage. Underline ten adverbial phrases of manner; then circle the prepositions in them. The first one is done for you.***

Although he is only eleven years old, James helps the aged. Every day, he goes (by) train to Redhill to help three old people there with shopping and housework. In this way, he has made their lives much easier.

It is through James' hard work that a Neighbourhood Care Programme was launched yesterday. James, with the help of his friends, has formed a group of young volunteers who seek out needy people. By their actions, these students have inspired others to join them. This band of willing volunteers treats old people with the utmost respect. They come by train, on foot, by bus and on bicycles to find out what they can do to make the lives of old people more comfortable. They do this without funding and without recognition. Their main aim is to make a difference through personal sacrifice. They are indeed very special people.

 ISBN 978-81-8477-750-5

E ***Look at the items on the shelves of Grandpa Green's shop. How would you explain where to find each item? Write three sentences using different adverbial phrases of place to explain their locations in relation to other objects. The box gives some adverbials you can use.***

in the corner	**on top of**	**in the centre of**
to the rear of	**at the back of**	**to the front of**
at the end of	**in between**	**within**
alongside	**close to**	**beside**
next to	**adjacent to**	**underneath**
to the left/right of	**on the first/second/third shelf**	

1. Do you have a kettle? Where can I find it?

   There is a kettle between the bowls and the iron on the second shelf.

   There is a kettle to the right of the bowls and next to the iron on the second shelf.

   There is a kettle above the electric fan.

2. Do you have an oven toaster? Where can I find it?

 ISBN 978-81-8477-750-5

3. Do you have any bowls? Where can I find them?

4. Do you have a rice cooker? Where can I find it?

5. Do you have any plates? Where can I find them?

6. Do you have an electric fan? Where can I find it?

7. Do you have any cane baskets? Where can I find them?

8. Do you have a radio? Where can I find it?

 ISBN 978-81-8477-750-5

8 Emphasizing and Comment Adverbs

Grammar Help

Some adverbs are used before adjectives or other adverbs to emphasize a point of view. For example: ***really, extremely, completely.***

- **Emphasizing adverbs** can be used to tell more about adjectives and adverbs as well.
- You can use a **comment adverb** (or **adverbial**) to express how you feel about something, or what your viewpoint is.

A ***Complete the sentences. You will need to decide whether to use an adjective or an adverb after the given emphasizing adverb in italics. Choose your word from the boxes below.***

Adverbs		Adjectives		
steadily highly	hard well	beautiful nervous	confident expressive	talented tired

Jan practised *awfully* (1) ____________ to win the music award. She was shaking and *extremely* (2) ____________ as she stepped onto the stage, even though she had worked *really* (3) ____________ all year. On the other hand, her mother, a piano teacher, was *completely* (4) ____________. She knew that Jan's technique was *exceptionally* (5) ____________ and she played *superbly* (6) ____________ in front of an audience. However, she also knew that Jane was *terribly* (7) ____________ from studying late. Despite her tiredness, Jan's playing that night was *extraordinarily* (8) ____________. The newspapers praised her *very* (9) ____________ and stated that she was *remarkably* (10) ____________.

 ISBN 978-81-8477-750-5

B ***Read the letter to the editor. Underline ten emphasizing adverbs. Write a V above the emphasizing adverb, if it emphasizes a verb; write Adj above it if it emphasizes an adjective, and Adv if it emphasizes an adverb.***

Dear Sir,

Our teacher told us of the Council's decision to drain Star Swamp completely and build a shopping centre in its place. We feel really strongly that this is a mistake. Star Swamp is a recreational area that students like us use for both leisure and science activities. By filling in the swamp, you will totally wipe out the home of many special native animals and birds. These animals rely entirely on humans to protect their natural habitat.

All the students in my class are quite aware of how important progress is, but it is extremely wrong to destroy our wildlife and green belt so thoughtlessly by building a shopping centre in such an exceptionally important area. Last year, our class spent three days of the holidays at Star Swamp—completely clearing away rubbish and destroying introduced weeds. This shows that we are absolutely committed to looking after the environment and we feel that it is just terrible that adults on the Council don't feel the same way.

Respectfully yours,

Andrew Lee

for Primary 5A

 ISBN 978-81-8477-750-5

Grammar Help

These are some **comment adverbs** and **adverbials** you can use for expressing your opinion.

Adverbs: ***naturally, admittedly, personally, unfortunately, seriously, hopefully, surely, preferably***

Adverbial phrases: ***in fairness, of course, no doubt, at least, in my opinion.***

C ***Complete the sentences below. They include a comment adverb to help you give your opinion.***

1. My sister likes science, but personally I ______________________________

____.

2. Mark had not studied and yet, unbelievably, ______________________

____

____.

3. Dark clouds are gathering. No doubt ______________________________

____.

4. Surprisingly ______________________________________

____.

5. Hopefully ____

____.

6. He said he wouldn't help us, but surely ____________________________

____

____.

 ISBN 978-81-8477-750-5

D ***Read the scenario below. Answer the questions by giving your point of view. Your answers must start with the adverbs provided.***

Robert was new to the neighbourhood. He was very shy and he found making friends difficult in his new school. One particular boy, Jim, was very mean to him. Every day he would tease Robert and take his pocket money by threatening to punch him.

Robert was not very big or muscular, but he had plenty of courage. One day, he decided he had had enough. He joined a kick-boxing class and began to train after school. He was determined to teach Jim a lesson he would never forget! The next time Jim tried to steal Robert's pocket money, he would go home with a black eye.

1. How is Robert feeling about the situation?

   Naturally, he ______________________________

   ____

2. What will happen if Robert stands up for himself?

   No doubt ______________________________

   ____

3. Is this a good way to tackle the problem?

   In my opinion, ______________________________

   ____

 ISBN 978-81-8477-750-5

4. What could happen to Robert?

   Unfortunately ______________________________

   ____

5. What will *definitely* happen in your opinion?

   Of course, ______________________________

   ____

6. Is there a better way for Robert to resolve this?

   Preferably he should ______________________________

   ____

7. How do you think this will end?

   Hopefully ______________________________

   ____

8. What do you think the teachers will do?

   Surely ______________________________

   ____

 ISBN 978-81-8477-750-5

9 Infinitives and Gerunds

Grammar Help

The **infinitive** is the base form of the verb. It often has **to** in front of it.

- It can follow another verb, for example: *We arranged **to meet** at the bus stop at 3:00 pm.*
- It can follow an object, for example: *The teacher told the children **to remain** in class after the bell.*
- It can follow an adjective, for example: *He was very happy **to see** his old friends again.*
- It can follow a noun or pronoun, for example: *I don't have any presents **to give**.*
- It often follows question words, for example: *I'm learning how **to knit**. I don't know what **to do**.*

There are lots of ways to use the **infinitive**.

- It can act as a noun, for example: ***To skate** is fun.* (= It is fun to skate.)
- It can act as an adjective, for example: *Mum had time **to spare**.* (= Mum had spare time.)
- It can act as an adverb, for example: *They were running **to escape**.* (Adverb of reason)

A ***Complete the following sentences by adding a to-infinitive. The first one is done for you.***

1. During the holidays, Sue learned how to bake cookies.
2. During the holidays, I've arranged ____________________
3. During the holidays, Jenny asked me ____________________
4. During the holidays, the boys were keen ____________________
5. During the holidays, I couldn't decide where ____________________
6. During the holidays, May persuaded me ____________________
7. During the holidays, they were hoping ____________________
8. During the holidays, John told us not ____________________

 ISBN 978-81-8477-750-5

B ***Write three sentences about the given topic. Use a verb that starts with to. An example has been given for each topic.***

1. Write about actions that you think are foolish things to do.

   It is foolish to cross a road without looking to see if there is traffic coming.

2. Write about three things you have tried hard to do.

   I have tried hard to keep my temper.

3. Write about three things you would like to do if you were able.

   If I had the money I would like to travel around the world.

4. Write about three things that are important for friends to do for each other.

   It is important for friends to help each other.

 ISBN 978-81-8477-750-5

Grammar Help

Some verbs end in **-ing** (**walking, sleeping**). These are called **present participles** and they are used to form the continuous tense.

Sometimes these **-ing** words are used as nouns: then they are called **gerunds.**

Sometimes an **-ing** word can be an adjective.

C ***Look at the way these -ing words are used in the following sentences. Circle the word in brackets that tells how the -ing words have been used.***

1. The delighted children were **laughing, playing** and **singing.** The *-ing* words in this sentence have been used as (adjectives / gerunds / present participles).
2. **Sailing** and **hiking** can be very strenuous sports. The *-ing* words in this sentence have been used as (adjectives / gerunds / present participles).
3. He put on his **running** shoes and **bowling** jacket. The *-ing* words in this sentence have been used as (adjectives / gerunds / present participles).
4. I love **riding** but I don't like walking. The *-ing* words in this sentence have been used as (adjectives / gerunds / present participles).
5. Dad was **weeding** and **fertilizing** the garden when I arrived home. The *-ing* words in this sentence have been used as (adjectives / gerunds / present participles).
6. We bought Dad a **skiing** pole for his birthday and a **walking** stick as a joke. The *-ing* words in this sentence have been used as (adjectives / gerunds / present participles).
7. The audience seems divided as some are **nodding** their heads and some are **shaking** theirs. The *-ing* words in this sentence have been used as (adjectives / gerunds / present participles).
8. **Running** and **skipping** were part of the children's daily exercise. The *-ing* words in this sentence have been used as (adjectives / gerunds / present participles).

 ISBN 978-81-8477-750-5

D ***Complete the following sentences using a suitable gerund from the box.***

exercising	**scrubbing**	**walking**
shopping	**painting**	**sailing**
reading	**skating**	**waiting**

1. The impatient man disliked ____________________.

2. If you live near the beach and have a boat, you probably like ____________________.

3. People who live in cold countries are often good at ____________________.

4. Sometimes doctors tell stressed patients to take up ____________________.

5. He is very artistic so ____________________ is his hobby.

6. There are many department stores in Singapore, so ____________________ is a favourite hobby.

7. He belongs to a gym because he knows that ____________________ is good for him.

8. I like clean floors and ____________________ keeps them nice and clean.

9. She is always at the library because ____________________ is her favourite pastime.

 ISBN 978-81-8477-750-5

E ***Look at the signs below and label them with a gerund that tells what is banned.***

1. No smoking ____________
2. ____________
3. ____________

4. ____________
5. ____________
6. ____________

7. ____________
8. ____________
9. ____________

 ISBN 978-81-8477-750-5

10 Prepositions and Phrasal Verbs

Grammar Help

Prepositions are small words that tell about place, time and direction. Some prepositions can be confused with adverbs. A preposition is always followed by a noun, pronoun or gerund (an **-ing** word that works as a noun), whereas an adverb gives more information about a verb.

A ***Complete the following personal recount using suitable prepositions from the box.***

for	in	along	at	after
to	by	from	on	until

A Visit to the Fire Station

Last Friday, our class visited the fire station to see how the Fire Department serves the community. We left school (1) ____________ 9:00 am, and travelled (2) ____________ one hour (3) ____________ bus (4) ____________ the highway (5) ____________ we reached the main fire station located (6) ____________ Green Street.

(7) ____________ arrival, we were met (8) ____________ the Fire Chief. He took us (9) ____________ a room where we watched a video (10) ____________ 10:00 am. (11) ____________ 11:00 am.

We were allowed to ask questions about what we had seen (12) ____________ the video. (13) ____________ that, we toured the station to see the fire engines and the firefighting equipment. We also

 ISBN 978-81-8477-750-5

visited the firefighters' quarters. I was allowed to put on a helmet

(14) ______________ a little while.

It was the best excursion we have been on this year.

Grammar Help

Prepositions are often combined with verbs, giving the verbs a special or different meaning. Such verbs are called **phrasal verbs**, for example: ***put on, break down, cover up.***

B ***Match the phrasal verb on the left to a verb that means the same on the right and write them in the space provided.***

1. blow up	• cancel	blow up = explode
2. bring back	• extinguish	______________
3. take on	• deliver	______________
4. put out	• start	______________
5. ring up	• delay	______________
6. put off	• suggest	______________
7. put forward	• refuse	______________
8. turn down	• employ	______________
9. call off	• explode	______________
10. bring over	• return	______________
11. take up	• phone	______________

 ISBN 978-81-8477-750-5

C ***Sometimes a phrasal verb can have different meanings. Read the different meanings of the phrasal verb "break down".***

> **break down** *phr v* (a) to stop working, to fail; (b) to lose control of one's feelings; (c) to separate or divide something into different parts; (d) to destroy, to knock to the ground

Decide which definition applies to each of the following sentences. The first one has been done for you.

1. The peace talks broke down because neither of the countries could agree on the terms.

   Definition (a)

2. The car broke down as we were travelling in Australia.

   ____

3. He broke down and cried as he read the sad story.

   ____

4. Can you give me a break down of the student population by age group, please?

   ____

5. After years of hard work, the old lady's health broke down.

   ____

6. "Open, or we'll break down the door," warned the police officer.

   ____

7. He will break down the information so that you can read it more easily.

   ____

8. The boy broke down and confessed when confronted by the evidence.

   ____

 ISBN 978-81-8477-750-5

D ***Select the correct phrasal verb from the box to complete each sentence.***

asked in
asked out
asked for

1. She was often ________________ by her many friends.
2. Oliver Twist ________________ some more food.
3. When strangers come to the door, they should never be ________________ .

closing in
closing up
closing down

4. The store was ________________ because of poor sales.
5. "Would you mind ________________ to make more space for others?"

cut up
cut off
cut out
cut down

6. The butcher ________________ the meat for her.
7. If you ________________ all the trees, you will ruin the land.
8. The council ________________ the water supply to repair the pipes.
9. The tailor must pin the cloth before he can ________________ the pattern.

set in
set up
set off
set out

10. The rain had really ________________ as they ________________ to climb the mountain. At the peak, they had to ________________ their tents for shelter, and ________________ their clothes to dry.

put off
put away
put back
put down

11. Children, ________________ those toys, pick up your clothes and ________________ them ________________ in the closet. You cannot ________________ cleaning your room any longer. Everything needs to be ________________ where it belongs.

 ISBN 978-81-8477-750-5

11 Modals: Obligation and Certainty

Grammar Help

Modals are words added to verbs to give information: to show how much we are obliged to do something.

- **Must** is used to show compulsion.
- **Should** and **ought** are used for advice, criticism and to express duty.

A ***Read each sign and write a sentence or two, as in the example, to show where you can find the sign and what it tells you. Be sure to use a modal in your answer.***

1. 
Passengers must not cross the tracks. Use the overhead bridge.

2. Patients should report to Reception on arrival.

3. To avoid delays, all cheques should be signed before approaching a teller.

4. Passengers in transit should proceed to the waiting lounge at Gate 5.

5. 
For the safety of all, dogs must be kept on leash.

6. Guests should not leave valuable items in their rooms. Safety deposit boxes are available at the Reception Desk.

7. 
Beware of pickpockets. Shoppers should ensure their wallets are secure.

8. 
Visitors shouldn't feed the monkeys. They are on a special diet.

 ISBN 978-81-8477-750-5

1. You must not cross the tracks at the train station. It is safer to use the overhead bridge.

2.

3.

4.

5.

6.

7.

8.

 ISBN 978-81-8477-750-5

B ***Write down something that you should remember to do. Use modals in your sentences.***

1. When I get up in the morning, ______________________________

____

2. When I arrive at school, ______________________________

____

3. When I arrive home from school, ______________________________

____

4. Before I go to bed, ______________________________

____

5. When someone gives me a present, ______________________________

____

6. When it's Mother's Day, ______________________________

____

7. When I accidentally upset my best friend, ______________________________

____

8. When I walk between two people in a crowd, ______________________________

____

Grammar Help

Modals such as **may**, **might**, **would** and **could** help us to discuss how much chance there is of something happening. They are generally used when we are not sure.

C ***Write a suitable reply to the question. Use a modal in your answer.***

1. Don't drop that wrapper on the floor. Where could you put it?

____

____

 ISBN 978-81-8477-750-5

2. Where might you go for your holiday?

3. What would happen if I can't play in the football finals?

4. What might you do if it snows?

5. What could I get my mum for a present?

6. How may I help you?

D ***Underline the modals in these riddles. Choose a suitable answer from the box and use the modal to help you write the answer. The first one is done for you.***

under a gorilla	**give him a hand**
a hot, cross bunny	**get a dingbat**
in the snow bank	**fish and ships**
eat it on Saturday	**when he loses his patience**

1. How could you cook toast in the jungle?

   You could cook it under a gorilla (griller).

2. What would you get if you poured boiling water down a rabbit hole?

3. What might sea monsters eat?

 ISBN 978-81-8477-750-5

4. What should you do for a starving cannibal?

____

5. What would you get if you crossed Dracula with a church bell?

____

6. Where might a Yeti keep his money?

____

7. How could you stop a cock from crowing and waking you on Sunday?

____

8. When must a doctor give up treating people?

____

Grammar Help

Different modals show different degrees (high, average, low) of certainty and obligation.

- **Must** (*must not/mustn't*), **shall** (*shall not/shan't*), **have to** (don't have to) are used when you are *very certain* about something, or *highly obliged* to do/not to do something.
- **Should** (*shouldn't*), **ought to** (*ought not to*), **can** (*cannot/can't*), **need to** (*need not to*) are used when you are *quite certain*, or *obliged* to do something.
- **May** (*may not*), **might** (*might not*), **could** (*could not*), **would** (*would not*) are used when you are *not very sure at all*, or when you are *not really obliged* to do something.

E ***Look at the list of occupations below.***

1. Put a star next to the ones that you might like to become and a cross next to those you would not choose.

mechanic	☐	**nurse**	☐	**teacher**	☐	**zookeeper**	☐
police officer	☐	**chef**	☐	**taxi driver**	☐	**ballet dancer**	☐

 ISBN 978-81-8477-750-5

2. Say why you want or don't want to do that occupation. Use modals to express the degree of certainty you feel and the obligations of the job.

Doctor: I shall not become a doctor. Doctors must work long hours and they have to give injections.

Veterinarian: I might become a veterinarian, because I would like to help animals.

(a) Mechanic: ______

(b) Police Officer: ______

(c) Ballet Dancer: ______

(d) Taxi Driver: ______

(e) Chef: ______

(f) Nurse: ______

(g) Teacher: ______

(h) Zookeeper: ______

 ISBN 978-81-8477-750-5

12 Simple Present and Simple Past Tenses

A ***Write three actions that are performed in the following places. You should use the present tense as these are habitual actions.***

1. At an airport: people greet each other, passengers board the planes, planes take off
2. at a restaurant: ______
3. on a farm: ______
4. at the beach: ______
5. at a football match: ______
6. in a library: ______
7. at the market: ______
8. at an athletics meet: ______

 ISBN 978-81-8477-750-5

B ***Read the poem and underline the verbs. Then rewrite the poem in the past tense as a recount by the climber, in the space provided below.***

Tree House

I take off my shoes and climb,
I clamber like a bear up the cedar tree.
Into the leafy crown I creep,
Higher and higher towards the beckoning sky,
Across rough branches that scrape my knees
Over twigs that prick and prod
Until I reach the safety of my tree house—
My sanctuary,
My refuge
That sways and bends to the will of the
wind
And becomes a pirate ship.
Or a dark, cool cave, or the depths of sea.
Here I stay wrapped in dreams until Mother calls,
"It's time for tea."

I took off my shoes and climbed, ______________________________

____

____

____

____

____

____

____

____

____

____

____

____

____

 ISBN 978-81-8477-750-5

C ***Imagine you are twenty years old. Read the list of things you might do now. Use this list to write simple past tense sentences that tell how your habits have changed. Use the example to help you.***

- I drive a car.
- I read books by Stephen King.
- I go to work.
- I wake up at 8:00.
- I dream of owning a plane.
- I exercise at a gym.
- I eat sashimi.

1. When I was young, I rode a bicycle. Now I drive a car.
2. ______________________________
3. ______________________________
4. ______________________________
5. ______________________________
6. ______________________________
7. ______________________________

 ISBN 978-81-8477-750-5

D ***Read the following description. It uses simple past tense to tell about habits in the old days.***

1. Underline the simple past tense verbs.

> Many people who lived in medieval times found life very difficult. The poorer people, called commoners or serfs, worked very hard. They slaved all day for lords or kings, who owned great stone castles, drank fine wine, dressed in delicate silks and ate off silver platters.
>
> Commoners paid the highest taxes. They could not afford to buy fine cloth, so they wore leather smocks, hard leather shoes, straw hats and rough shirts and pants. They farmed small plots of land and sold a little grain. They lived in shacks made of mud, sticks, straw and wood. Craftsmen, who made candles, shoes and furniture for the wealthy, had a much better life than the commoners. Their guilds protected and helped them.
>
> Not many people travelled in those days, so minstrels moved from town to town to pass on the news, which was often sung rather than told, to the people. When a minstrel arrived, the lord or king held a banquet, at which food was provided for everyone in the castle.

2. Write three short sentences about your life as if you were living in the medieval times. An example is done for you.

(a) I am a craftsman. I make shoes for the king. I belong to a guild. I earn money making shoes for people.

(b) I am a serf. ______________________________

____

(c) I am a minstrel. ______________________________

____

(d) I am the king of a castle. ______________________________

____

 ISBN 978-81-8477-750-5

13 Present Continuous Tense

Grammar Help

The **present continuous tense** is used when an action is taking place at the time you are speaking about it.

You use **am/is/are** + a **present participle** to form the tense. For example:
I **am watching** television. We **are having** a lot of fun.

A ***Look at these pictures. Each person is miming an action. What do you think the person is doing? Write a sentence about it, using the present continuous tense. The first one is done for you.***

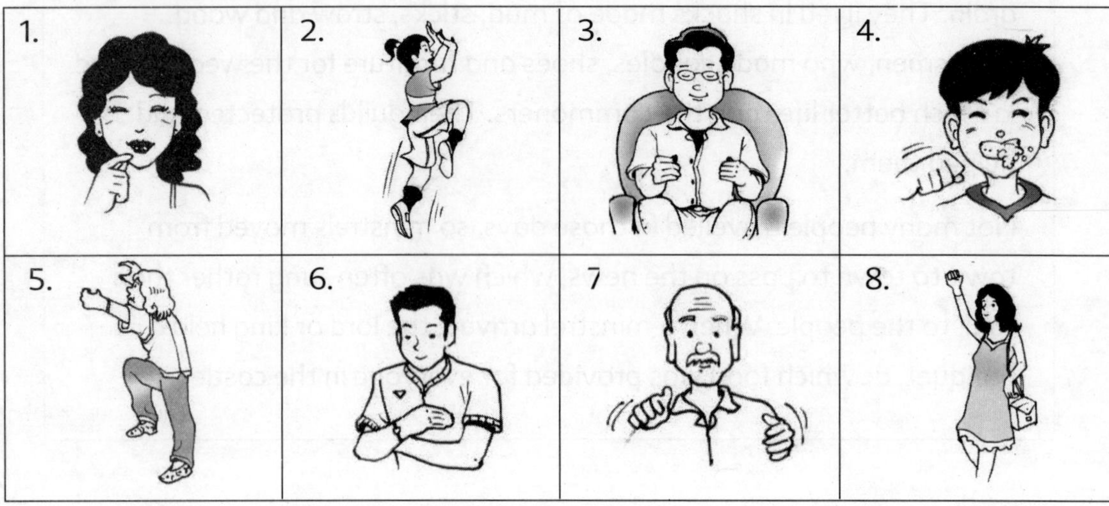

1. I think the woman is putting on her lipstick.
2. ______
3. ______
4. ______
5. ______
6. ______
7. ______
8. ______

 ISBN 978-81-8477-750-5

B ***John is always making excuses when his father tells him to do his homework. He always tells him he is doing something else. Write down four excuses that you think he might use.***

John, it's time you started your homework.

1. I can't just yet, Dad. I'm feeding the dog.

2. ______________________

3. ______________________

4. ______________________

5. ______________________

C ***Complete the text below by adding present continuous tense verbs made from the words in the box.***

toss	blare	pray	sleep	try	yell	yowl	rattle

It's a sweltering night and I (1) ______________________ to get to sleep. Unfortunately, something (2) ______________________ at my window and next door's cat (3) ______________________. The streets are busy, so car horns (4) ______________________ and impatient drivers (5) ______________________ at each other. I cannot sleep, so I (6) ______________________ and turning. I (7) ______________________ that the noise will stop soon so I can get to sleep. My lucky parents (8) ______________________ already.

 ISBN 978-81-8477-750-5

D ***Look at each picture and use the present continuous tense to answer the question. You should give a possible reason for the action.***

Why are they digging?

1. The pirate is hiding his treasure.
2. ______________________________
3. ______________________________
4. ______________________________

Why are they running?

5. ______________________________
6. ______________________________
7. ______________________________
8. ______________________________

Why are they laughing?

9. ______________________________
10. ______________________________
11. ______________________________
12. ______________________________

 ISBN 978-81-8477-750-5

Grammar Help

These adverbs and adverbials are used with the present continuous tense to emphasize that the action is on-going: **still, at present, at the moment, now, just.**

E ***Use the ideas and adverbials in the brackets to complete Suzy's part of this dialogue.***

Salesman : Hello, little girl. Can I speak to your mother?

Suzy : Sorry, Mother's busy. She (1) ______________________

(dinner, at present)

Salesman : Then, can I talk to your father?

Suzy : Dad's not free. He (2) ______________________

(bath, just)

Salesman : How about your older brother or sister?

Suzy : That's no good. Brother (3) ______________________

(phone, girlfriend, still)

Salesman : Isn't there anyone I can talk to ?

Suzy : Well, you (4) ______________________, aren't you? (me, now)

 ISBN 978-81-8477-750-5

14 Present Perfect Tense

Grammar Help

The **present perfect tense** is formed from the verb **has/have** + a **past participle.** (For singular subjects you use **has.** For plural subjects you use **have.**)

The present perfect tense has three main uses:

- To talk about something that began in the past but still has an effect now. For example: *I **have lived** in Singapore for seven years. I **have waited** since three o'clock for you to come.* This function often includes the words **since** (followed by a time or date) and **for** (followed by a number).
- To talk about things done during a person's life. For example: ***Have** you ever **ridden** on an elephant? No, I **have** never **ridden** on an elephant.* This function often includes the words **ever**, **always** and **never**.
- To talk about events that are recently completed. For example: *Mum **has** already **prepared** the dinner. I **have** just **missed** my bus.* This function often includes adverbs such as **just** and **already**.

A ***Use the present perfect tense to write down what you think has happened. The first one is done for you.***

1. Jack, who loves playing soccer, is using crutches and his leg is covered in plaster.

   Jack has broken his leg playing soccer.

2. All the girls in the school netball team are smiling and holding up a trophy.

   ____

3. Dad, whose clothes are wet, is emptying a bucket and admiring his clean car.

   ____

4. At the station, Ben is panting and perspiring while he watches the train pull away.

   ____

 ISBN 978-81-8477-750-5

5. Sue has dirt on her knees and there is a pile of weeds next to the flowerbed.

6. The chocolate box is empty and Jan's dog, Spot, is nosing some wrappers on the ground.

7. Bob's face is red, his T-shirt is too big and he's perspiring. He's wearing jogging shoes.

8. There is glass all over the floor, the painting is ruined, and the hook on the wall is missing.

9. The window is broken and Madam Lim's ruby necklace is missing.

Grammar Help

The present perfect tense often uses time markers (or adverbs) such as **just**, **yet**, **already**, **still**, **always**, **ever** and **never**.

Sometimes these time markers, like **already**, **always** or **just**, come between **has/have** and the past participle. Negative words, like **not** or **never**, also come between **has/have** and the past participle.

 ISBN 978-81-8477-750-5

B ***Match the sentence beginning on the left with a suitable present perfect tense verb in the centre column and a sentence ending on the right. Write the sentence you have made on the lines provided.***

1. My sister	• have just arrived	• their best to excel this year.
2. My parents	• has already left	• us since last August.
3. A few students	• have not tried	• reading glasses to read his paper.
4. The music students	• has always played	• at the new restaurant yet.
5. My favourite aunt	• has never needed	• in Australia for very long.
6. Jane	• have not eaten	• the station.
7. Sam, a keen reader,	• has not visited	• tennis on Sundays.
8. The train	• has not lived	• all the books in the class library.
9. My old uncle	• has already read	• in the hall with their instruments.

1. ______________________________

____

2. ______________________________

____

3. ______________________________

____

4. ______________________________

____

5. ______________________________

____

 ISBN 978-81-8477-750-5

6. ______________________________

____

7. ______________________________

____

8. ______________________________

____

9. ______________________________

____

C ***Look at what Mother said. Write down two possible reasons she would have for saying what she did. Use present perfect tense verbs with the time marker given. An example has been given for each one.***

1. Don't come inside.
Time marker: just

(a) I have just washed the floor.

(b) ______________________________

____

2. You are so unreliable.
Time marker: yet

(a) You haven't washed the dishes yet.

(b) ______________________________

____

3. Now I can relax.
Time marker: already

(a) I have already hung the washing.

(b) ______________________________

____

 ISBN 978-81-8477-750-5

4. I'm very angry with you.
Time marker: still

(a) You still have not cleaned your room.

(b)

5. Your new friend is very different.
Time marker: never

(a) He has never eaten meat before.

(b)

D ***The list shows the chores that Kathy has done and those she still has to do. Write sentences about them using the present perfect tense and suitable time markers from the box. You must use each marker in at least one sentence.***

still	already	just	yet

To-do List	Done
- Water plants	
- Wash dishes	
- Feed cat	
- Sweep floor	
- Turn out cupboard	
- Cut vegetables	
- Drink up milk	
- Buy bread	

1. Kathy has just watered the plants.
2. She has not washed the dishes yet.

 ISBN 978-81-8477-750-5

3. ______________________________

____

4. ______________________________

____

5. ______________________________

____

6. ______________________________

____

7. ______________________________

____

8. ______________________________

____

 ISBN 978-81-8477-750-5

15 Past Continuous Tense

Grammar Help

You use **was/were** + a **present participle** to form the **past continuous tense**. This tense can be used to tell about:

- an action that was going on when something else happened.
  For example: *I **was sleeping** when the siren sounded.*
- an action that was taking place for some time in the past.
  For example: *We **were watching** a show last night.*
- two actions that were taking place at the same time.
  For example: *Mary **was writing** while her brother **was washing** the dishes.*

A ***Look at the pictures and use the past continuous tense to answer the question on what the people were doing. The first one is done for you.***

What were they doing when the phone rang?

1.

2.

3.

4.

1. I was having a bath when the phone rang.
2. They ______
3. Mark ______
4. He ______

 ISBN 978-81-8477-750-5

What was Dad doing when the electricity failed?

5. Dad ______________________

6. He ______________________

7. He ______________________

B ***Look at the pictures. Complete each sentence using the past continuous form of the verb given.***

1. Last Sunday, they ______________________
____
____
(picnic)

2. Last evening, we ______________________
____
____
(wait)

3. Half an hour ago, we ______________________
____
____
(walk)

 ISBN 978-81-8477-750-5

C ***Read the play script below. Fill in each blank with the past continuous form of the verb in brackets.***

Detective : You are all suspects in this robbery. Tell me what you (1) ______________ (do) at nine o'clock last Sunday morning.

Suspect 1 : I was home with my wife. We (2) ______________ (work) in the garden. We (3) ______________ (dig) up the old garden bed. You can ask the neighbours. They (4) ______________ (garden) also. They (5) ______________ (plant) tomatoes.

Suspect 2 : I (6) ______________ (play) golf at the country club, when the robbery (7) ______________ (take) place. I think I (8) ______________ (putt) the sixth hole about that time. You can ask the club professional. He (9) ______________ (help) me to improve my game.

Suspect 4 : I guess I'm the main suspect then, because I (10) ______________ (watch) soccer at home. My wife (11) ______________ (shop) in the mall. No one (12) ______________ (keep) me company.

Detective : No, you're not the main suspect. The thief (13) ______________ (wear) size 12 shoes and your shoe size is smaller than that.

 ISBN 978-81-8477-750-5

Grammar Help

The **past continuous form** of a verb often occurs with words like **while, when** and **as**. These are used to tell about two actions that are going on at the same time in the past.

D ***Last week, Tom saw an accident. The police officer who attended the scene asked Tom to fill in a witness report. Help Tom to complete the report by circling the more appropriate tense of the two.***

I (**1** was walking / walked) along Orchard Road, when I saw a boy in a blue T-shirt come out of the train station. I (**2** was wearing / wore) my sunglasses because the sun (**3** was shining / shone) very brightly and it was difficult to see properly without them. I don't think the boy could see very well because he (**4** was squinting / squinted) at the bright light. He (**5** was walking / walked) briskly towards the crosswalk, and I saw that the cars (**6** were moving / moved) very fast. A few cars (**7** were waiting / waited) to turn left, but I don't think the boy (**8** was seeing / saw) them. He stepped off the kerb just as a silver Mercedes (**9** was turning / turned) the corner, and the car (**10** was hitting / hit) him. The boy (**11** was lying / lay) on the road when the driver, who (**12** was trembling / trembled) with shock, (**13** was touching / touched) him. I felt sorry for the boy, but the driver was not at fault. The boy didn't see the red "don't walk" sign because the sun (**14** was glaring / glared) in his eyes.

 ISBN 978-81-8477-750-5

E ***Suzanne has had a bad week. These are some of the things that happened to her from Monday to Friday. Write sentences describing her weekdays.***

1. On Monday, as Suzanne was dancing on stage, she tripped and fell over.
2.
3.
4.
5.

 ISBN 978-81-8477-750-5

16 Past Perfect Tense

Grammar Help

The past perfect tense is formed by using **had** + a past participle: ***had forgotten***, ***had eaten***. It is used:

- to talk about an event or action that was completed before another past event. It is used with words like **before**, **when** and **after**.
  For example: *She had lived in Japan before she moved to Singapore.*
- to refer to an earlier time in the past. When you talk about a time in the past, you use the simple past tense, but if you want to refer to a time even earlier than that time, you use the past perfect.
  For example: *All the crops* ***were ruined*** *by the time the rains* ***had arrived***. (**were ruined** is the event that happened first, **had arrived** is the later event)
- with the conditional **if** to show that something didn't happen (*If only you had told me earlier*). Conditional sentences usually include **could have**, **would have** or **might have**. For example: *If I had known you were coming, I would have baked a cake.*
- in reported speech, where the present perfect tense is changed to the past perfect.

A ***Underline all the past perfect verbs in the following passage.***

Peter and Paul had become best friends as soon as they had enrolled at their new school. Peter had travelled from Australia with his family and Paul had arrived from England. Both of their fathers had transferred to Singapore, so the boys had been forced to leave their school friends and move with their families. They had been very nervous on the first day, until they met each other in the school canteen. Since that day, they had caught the same train to school and had played together every day.

 ISBN 978-81-8477-750-5

B ***Put the verbs, shown in brackets, into the past perfect form.***

1. After he ____________________ (plant) the seedlings, the gardener raked the leaves.
2. Before Ann could open her umbrella, it ____________________ (start) to rain.
3. When the police arrived, the thief ____________________ (leave) already.
4. By 7:00 pm, Dan ____________________ (eat) his dinner and left the restaurant.
5. They were ushered to their seats after they ____________________ (show) their tickets.
6. I bought the new jeans after I ____________________ (try) them on for size.
7. They stopped playing after their mother ____________________ (call) them in for lunch.
8. The pod of dolphins ____________________ (swim) away by the time the Greenpeace boat reached the oil slick.

C ***Mr Jones' garage has a checklist for all mechanics. Bob, the new apprentice, is not very good at his job. Write sentences saying what he did and what he did not do. Use the past perfect tense to show the actions he had completed before he did or did not do the next action.***

1 ✓ start car	4 ✓ fill in new oil
☐ listen to engine	☐ top up radiator
2 ✓ observe exhaust emission	5 ✓ start car again
✓ turn off engine	✓ tune engine
3 ✓ drain off oil	6 ✓ shake out mats
☐ check spark plugs	✓ vacuum car inside

1. After Bob had started the car, he did not listen to the engine.

 ISBN 978-81-8477-750-5

2. ______________________________

____

3. ______________________________

____

4. ______________________________

____

5. ______________________________

____

6. ______________________________

____

D ***The past perfect can be used in an adverbial clause of reason. Complete each sentence using the past perfect form to tell why this happened.***

1. She began to cry because she had missed her train.
2. He returned home from school early because ______________________________

____
3. She didn't want to go sailing because ______________________________
4. She received excellent marks in the test because ______________________________

____
5. The dog barked loudly because ______________________________
6. She was very hungry because ______________________________
7. My friend won a scholarship because ______________________________
8. He came as quickly as he could because ______________________________

____

 ISBN 978-81-8477-750-5

Grammar Help

When you change direct speech to reported speech, the present perfect tense in direct speech changes to **past perfect**. For example:
*"I **have** never **seen** such excellent work," said the teacher.*
becomes: *The teacher said that she **had** never **seen** such excellent work.*

In reported speech, pronouns usually change from first or second person to third person. For example: *"We haven't been there before," he said.*
becomes: *He said they hadn't been there before.*

E ***Change what the person is saying into reported speech. Use the starting words given. The first one is done for you.***

1. He said that he had read that book already. ______ — I've read that book already.
2. June told me that ______ ______ — My sister has caught chicken pox.
3. Mary asked me ______ ______ — What has happened to change your mind?
4. Jill demanded to know ______ ______ — Who has taken my ruler?
5. Miss Lee reminded us that ______ ______ — You have left a mess in the art room.
6. He explained that ______ ______ — I have been suffering from the flu.
7. Mr Pereira warned me that ______ ______ — I have had enough of your nonsense.
8. John said that ______ ______ — I have seen that movie already.
9. Sue yelled excitedly that ______ ______ — The mail has arrived!

 ISBN 978-81-8477-750-5

F ***Look at the picture. Use it to make guesses why the children decided to go into this spooky house. The prompts and the verbs should help you. Give as much information as you can in your sentences.***

1. Kitten (had seen) They had seen a small kitten that needed rescuing.
2. Dog (had chased) ______________________
3. Parcel (had asked) ______________________
4. Weather (had rained) (had wanted) ______________________
5. Old man (had fallen) ______________________
6. Umbrella (had blown) (had snagged) ______________________
7. Pile of leaves (had caught) ______________________

 ISBN 978-81-8477-750-5

17 Talking About the Future

Grammar Help

The **future tense** refers to an action that hasn't happened yet, but will happen in the future. To talk about the future, you can use:

- the simple future—**shall** and **will**, for example: *She **will come** tomorrow.*
- **going to**, for example: *I **am going** to Australia in December.*
- the simple present, for example: *Tomorrow **is** my birthday.*
- the present continuous, for example: *She **is holding** a party for her birthday next month.*
- the structure **be** + **about to** + verb, for example: *Hurry, the train **is about to leave**.*

A ***Read the dialogue below. Underline the verbs that talk about actions that will happen some time in the future.***

It's Saturday morning and Ms Lee is trying to arrange a meeting for some customers. Her manager, Mr Ross, is very busy so it is difficult to find a suitable time.

Mr Ross : I can't see them now, Ms Lee. I'm about to leave the office. My wife and I will be visiting Indonesia this weekend.

Ms Lee : Then how about eight o'clock on Monday? I'll come in early on Monday.

Mr Ross : No, I'm sorry, I can't. I'm attending an all-day seminar on Monday. The people who'll be at the seminar are very important contacts. After that I'm going to take my wife to dinner. It's her birthday on Monday.

Ms Lee : Hmm, I see you are going to be free between ten and eleven on Tuesday. Shall I make it 10:15 in the morning, then?

Mr Ross : I'm afraid not. I'm about to sign an important contract. I shall need time to read it properly.

 ISBN 978-81-8477-750-5

Ms Lee : Then, what are you doing on Wednesday?

Mr Ross : I'm entertaining overseas visitors in the morning. Mr Brown arrives from Australia at 10:00 am. Later, my wife and I plan to take him to lunch.

Ms Lee : Mr Ross, my customers are not going to wait for another whole week. They'll cancel their order.

Mr Ross : Yes, you're right. Tell them I'll see them on Wednesday at four in the afternoon. I must leave to pick up my wife, so I'll see you on Monday. Goodbye, Ms Lee.

B ***Answer these questions. Follow the tense form used in the question.***

1. Where are you going in the holidays?

___

2. How will you get there?

___

3. Who are you going to see there?

___

4. What are you going to do there?

___

5. Where do you think you will be living in ten years' time?

___

6. What do you think your occupation is going to be?

___

7. What countries do you think you will visit when you are grown up?

___

 ISBN 978-81-8477-750-5

Grammar Help

The **present continuous tense** is used to show future action when we have already made definite plans. (This is slightly different from the 'going to' form.)

C ***Look at Jane's diary. Complete the dialogue explaining why she can't visit Jenny. Use the present continuous tense in your answers.***

SUNDAY	
7:00	jogging with Dad (Botanic Gardens)
8:00 +	Help Mum with the shopping (market)
9:00	
10:00	visit Grandma with the family
11:00	
12:00	Birthday lunch for Grandma
1:00	
2:00	
3:00	Sally's birthday party at McDonalds
4:00	
5:00	return books to Tom (5:30)
6:00	Dinner (if I'm hungry!)
Evening	baby sitting for the Lee family 7—10 pm

Jenny : Why not come over early, say at 8:30 am?

Jane : (1) I'm helping Mum with the shopping, so I can't come at 8:30 am.

Jenny : OK, then perhaps you can come at ten.

Jane : (2) ____________________

____

 ISBN 978-81-8477-750-5

Jenny : Well, how about half-past eleven instead? You could stay for lunch.

Jane : (3) ______________________________

____

Jenny : Let's make it three o'clock then.

Jane : (4) ______________________________

____

Jenny : How about five o'clock? The party should be over by then.

Jane : (5) ______________________________

____

Jenny : Oh, what about after you've seen Tom, say around 6:00 pm?

Jane : (6) ______________________________

____

Jenny : I'll still be up at nine. Why don't you come then?

Jane : (7) ______________________________

____

Jenny : It looks as though this Sunday is impossible. Let's make it next week, then.

D ***Here are some scenarios. Underline any present continuous verbs used in the scenarios. Then write two sentences to describe what you think is about to happen. The first one is done for you.***

A small village town is located at the base of a tall mountain. Smoke is coming from the top of the mountain. Residents are packing their valuables.

1. The mountain is a volcano that is about to erupt.
2. The people are about to evacuate the village.

 ISBN 978-81-8477-750-5

The children don't have school for four weeks. The Brown family have packed their rods and bait. Mrs Brown is making a picnic lunch and filling flasks. It's 4:00 am.

3. The holidays ______________________________

4. The Brown family ______________________________

Three boys are standing outside the Principal's office. One of the boys has a black eye and another has a bruise on his cheek. The boys are feeling very nervous because they know they have broken a rule.

5. The boys ______________________________

6. They ______________________________

Janet is 21 years old. She is very excited, but also very nervous. She is wearing a smart suit and is clutching a briefcase that her parents gave her as a present. This will be her first day.

7. Janet ______________________________

The crowd is very tense. Time is almost up. The players are lined up on the keyway and the scores are even. John is panting from the effort. His eyes are fixed on the back board.

8. The basketball final ______________________________

9. John ______________________________

Kim and Robert are in a church. Kim is dressed in a long white dress. Some of her family and friends are crying. Robert has on a tuxedo. He is standing next to his best friend. A small boy is carrying a satin pillow with two rings.

10. Kim and Robert ______________________________

 ISBN 978-81-8477-750-5

18 Direct and Indirect Objects

Grammar Help

The **subject** of a sentence is the person (or thing) the sentence is about. When the subject does something to another person (or thing), that person (or thing) is called the **object**. For example: *Mum* (subject) *is reading* ***the newspaper*** (object).

- An easy way to identify the object is to ask, "What or who?" after the verb.
- Objects can come in a variety of forms. For example: *I enjoy* ***sitting in the sun****. I want* ***to go home now****.*

A ***The sentences below have only one object. Circle the verb and underline the direct object in each sentence.***

1. John plays the trombone in the school band.
2. Mrs Lee wants a new car for her birthday.
3. In school today, we wrote a report about Africa.
4. I don't want to borrow this book.
5. Every week, Su-Lin visits her grandmother.
6. The guard dog chased the thief.
7. My aunt is knitting a scarf for winter.
8. The birds are building a nest in the tree.

 ISBN 978-81-8477-750-5

B ***Circle the main verbs and underline the direct objects in the following short recount. Can you find at least eight objects? The first one is done for you.***

Benjamin Franklin

Benjamin Franklin, a famous American, invented many things. He wrote books and also worked as a diplomat. He is considered one of American history's most famous statesmen.

Born in 1706, Benjamin Franklin shared his childhood with many brothers and sisters. In fact, he was the seventeenth child in his family. Like most children in those days, he only attended school for two years. He learnt his father's trade—soap and candle making—for two years; then apprenticed himself to his brother, a printer. He also started to write articles and tricked his brother into printing them. When he was twenty-three, Franklin wrote and printed his own newspaper.

In 1747, Franklin began experimenting with electricity. He invented the lightning rod and discovered two kinds of electricity—positive and negative. He taught himself many foreign languages and later set up a college, which is today's University of Pennsylvania. He went on to become one of the greatest statesmen America has ever known. Benjamin Franklin died in 1790, aged 84.

C ***Add a direct object to complete the following sentences.***

1. The anxious crowd watched ____________________
2. The painters have finished ____________________
3. The boy is reading ____________________
4. The policemen will check ____________________
5. Mother buys ____________________
6. The waitress brought ____________________

 ISBN 978-81-8477-750-5

Grammar Help

Sometimes a sentence can have two objects. The main object is called the **direct object** because the verb refers directly to it. The second object is called the **indirect object**. For example: *Jack gave* ***me*** (indirect object) *a* ***birthday gift*** (direct object).

- When two objects are used, the indirect object always comes before the direct object.
- Indirect objects are always people or animals, and very often pronouns are used.

D ***Underline the direct object in these sentences.***
Circle the other object.
Rewrite the sentence so that the indirect object is put before the direct object.

1. Mother buys flowers for Grandma.

____

2. The waitress brought the menu to us.

____

3. The company gave a gold watch to Sam.

____

4. Mother showed the broken cup to Daisy and told her to be more careful.

____

____

5. Dan is catching a butterfly for his sister.

____

____

 ISBN 978-81-8477-750-5

E ***Look at the pictures and words. Write about what the family members and pets are doing or have done. Some sentences will have direct objects and some will have both direct and indirect objects.***

is glancing at	**is feeding**
has knitted	**is giving**
is writing	**has baked**
is drawing	**is scratching**

1. Mother ____

2. Father ____

3. Grandma ______________________________________

4. Ben ____

5. Grandpa ______________________________________

6. The cat ______________________________________

7. Aunt Susan ___________________________________

8. May ____

 ISBN 978-81-8477-750-5

19 Transitive and Intransitive Verbs

Grammar Help

A verb is **transitive** when it takes an object. It is **intransitive** when it has no object.

For intransitive verbs, the action is confined to the doer (the subject). It does not pass over to an object.

Some verbs, like **ache** and **touch down**, are always intransitive.

A ***Read this part of a narrative and circle at least five transitive verbs. Write "I" above the intransitive verbs. Underline the object of each of your circled verbs.***

The blacksmith lifted the heavy hammer high into the air. It descended swiftly and struck the anvil with a metallic ringing sound. The red-hot iron bent easily. He flexed his muscles again, raised the hammer skywards and smashed the iron bar into the shape he wanted. Then he paused. Quickly the young apprentice lad handed his master a glass of ale.

The gigantic man drank thirstily and wiped his mouth with the back of his hand. Critically, he studied the horseshoe he was making. It was a fine shoe; fit for a fine horse. He grunted contentedly and threw the horseshoe into a wooden box with the other three he had made. Tomorrow he would collect his money from the squire.

 ISBN 978-81-8477-750-5

B ***Underline the verb. Put a tick next to the sentence with a transitive verb and a cross next to the one with an intransitive verb.***

1. The sound of the orchestra echoed through the concert hall. ☐
2. The old man took off his coat. ☐
3. The rich man drove an expensive car. ☐
4. The bus arrived ten minutes late. ☐
5. Her library contained many books. ☐
6. The posters were hung on the south wall. ☐
7. The naughty child broke his mother's best plate. ☐
8. Sue nominated her best friend for Head Prefect. ☐
9. The students read silently during the assembly period. ☐
10. Due to the cold weather, we stayed in class during break time. ☐

C ***These sentences are not complete because they contain transitive verbs, but no object. Add an object to show what each person does.***

1. A coachman drives ________________________.
2. An optician tests ________________________.
3. A charwoman cleans ________________________.
4. A philatelist collects ________________________.
5. A veterinarian treats ________________________.
6. A pharmacist prepares and dispenses ________________________.
7. An archaeologist studies ________________________.
8. A taxidermist preserves and stuffs ________________________.

 ISBN 978-81-8477-750-5

D ***Many verbs can be both transitive and intransitive. Underline the phrasal verbs in the sentences below and decide whether they are transitive or intransitive. Write "I" for intransitive and "T" for transitive in the space.***

1.	The plane took off very late. ____	He took off his coat and tie. ____
2.	Someone broke into the house. ____	A tramp broke in and made a mess. ____
3.	John turned on the light. ____	The canoe turned over in the rapids. ____
4.	She stood out in a crowd. ____	John stood for elections. ____
5.	We got away after an hour. ____	The thief got away with the jewels. ____
6.	The injection will wear off soon. ____	Don't wear out my patience. ____
7.	Hang onto the rope or you'll fall. ____	Please volunteer—don't hang back. ____
8.	Look out! That car is speeding! ____	Help me look for a phone, please. ____

Grammar Help

The transitive verb **to lay** (= to set something down) is often confused with the intransitive verb **to lie** (= to stretch out; the past tense form is **lay**).

E ***Complete the following sentences by choosing whether the missing verb is transitive or intransitive. Choose the best verb form from the box for the blank.***

lay	**is/are lying**	**lie**	**is/are laying**
has ... laid	**laid**	**has ... lain**	**lay**

1. Birds ____________________ eggs, but decorators ____________________ carpets.

 ISBN 978-81-8477-750-5

2. The tourists __________ in the sun despite skin cancer warnings.

3. The plumbers __________ the new pipes.

4. __________ down and listen to the wind in the trees.

5. Rover __________ panting in the shade after the long walk.

6. My pet hen __________ just __________ an egg in my bag.

7. Mother __________ just __________ down for a quick rest before dinner.

8. I __________ the table yesterday; it's your turn today.

F ***Some sentences have both direct and indirect objects. Complete the table by adding suitable verbs and objects for the blanks. Underline the direct object.***

Subject	Verb	Indirect Object	Direct Object
My mother		my brother	a birthday cake.
Julian		me	his pen.
Sara		her father	a kiss goodbye.
The school board			
The zookeeper			fruit.
Dad			tickets to the final.
The monkey			
The mayor			
Doctor Wang			
The sun			

 ISBN 978-81-8477-750-5

20 Connectors and Conjunctions

Grammar Help

Connectors are used to link two ideas together to make your meaning clearer. They let you compare and contrast information more easily. **Conjunctions** are a special kind of connector; they help you to join two clauses together.

- The conjunctions **as, since, because, for** and **in case** are used to give reasons. They introduce the explanation that answers the question 'Why?'
- The conjunctions **so that, in order that** and **in case** and the connectors **so as to** and **in order to** are used to state a purpose. They introduce the answer to the question 'What for?'
- The conjunctions **if, unless** and **as long as** are used to introduce conditions.
- If the phrase or clause with the connector comes at the beginning of the sentence, you should put a comma to separate it from the main clause.

A ***Match each sentence beginning with a suitable reason from the box. Copy the clause on the lines provided and underline the conjunction that shows reason.***

since his cousin was coming to stay.
for all the arrangements she had to make.
as she wanted to invite his cousin also.
in case her friends had made other plans.
because it was her birthday.
because she had planned well.
so she could organise everything.
as it was too late to post invitations.

1. Jenny decided to have a party ________________________________

2. She phoned to ask her friends to come ____________________________

____

 ISBN 978-81-8477-750-5

3. Benson decided not to go ______________________________

4. She rang Benson again ______________________________

5. Jenny was worried ______________________________

6. She couldn't sleep ______________________________

7. On the day of the party, she woke up early ______________________________

____

8. The party was a success ______________________________

B ***Look at the actions listed below. Decide on the reason for each person acting this way; then write a sentence about it. Be sure to include one of the following conjunctions: because, since, as, for, in case.***

1. He caught the train, not the plane.

   He caught the train as he wanted to see the mountain scenery.

2. She didn't want to wear the dress her mother bought her.

   ____

3. They didn't go to school today.

   ____

4. They paid a higher price for their tickets.

   ____

5. She didn't have any dinner.

   ____

6. The students ran for shelter.

   ____

 ISBN 978-81-8477-750-5

C *Match each sentence beginning in the first column with a suitable purpose or condition in the second column. Write the complete sentence on the lines provided and underline the connectors.*

1. As long as the weather stays fine,	• store some food for the journey.
2. Dad had the car serviced at the garage so that	• it rains.
3. Mum bought a new picnic basket in order to	• be ready well before we leave.
4. We plan to leave on Saturday, unless	• we plan to drive to Malacca.
5. We might stay overnight, if	• the brakes would be reliable.
6. I'm packing early so as to	• be ready for any emergencies.
7. Mum's packing a first aid kit in order to	• we can find a cheap motel.

1. ______________________________

____

2. ______________________________

____

3. ______________________________

____

4. ______________________________

____

5. ______________________________

____

6. ______________________________

____

7. ______________________________

____

 ISBN 978-81-8477-750-5

D ***Add a comma to each sentence to separate the main clause from the phrase or clause with the connector. Say what kind of connector it is—Reason, Purpose or Condition.***

1. Since she did not want to upset her mother Mae Lin did not go to the party. ________
2. As long as his father was in hospital William was not going out. ________
3. Because she had homework Kim came home early from the party. ________
4. In order to complete his homework John came home early from the party. ________
5. Unless her mother allowed her Sue was not going to the party. ________
6. As Bob couldn't dance he came home from the party early. ________
7. If she could leave early Pat would go to the party. ________
8. In case his father needed him Andrew came home early from the party. ________

Grammar Help

Adverbs of time and sequence, such as **when, before, after, until** (**till**), **since, as soon as, while** and **next** can act as conjunctions to tell about a sequence of events.

E ***Use the time conjunctions given in the numbered sentence beginnings on the next page to tell the story shown in the pictures. The numbers in the pictures match the sentences. Use the words in the box in some of your sentences.***

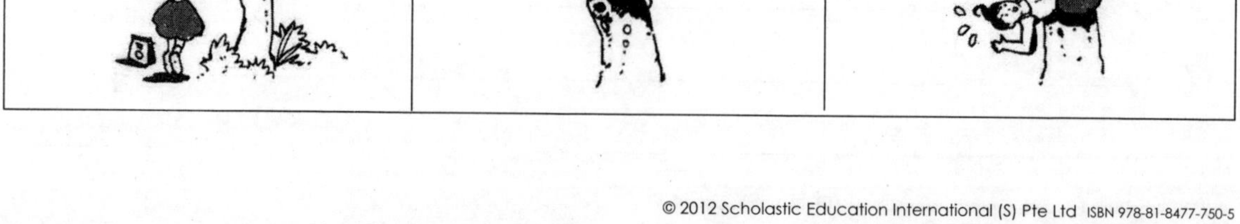

 ISBN 978-81-8477-750-5

4. 

5. 

6. 

7. 

8. 

9. 

coax **ran out of ideas** **fire brigade**

The Rescue

Before breakfast, Susan went out into the garden, where she saw a small kitten up a tree. The kitten was trembling and too frightened to climb down, so Susan decided to rescue it.

1. First she ______________________________
2. Then she ______________________________
3. While ______________________________
4. Next, she tried ______________________________
5. Finally, ______________________________
6. When ______________________________
7. Then Susan ______________________________
8. Before long ______________________________
9. As soon as ______________________________

 ISBN 978-81-8477-750-5

21 More Connectors

Grammar Help

Conjunctions are a form of connector because they are used to link two clauses together.

- The conjunctions ***if... then***, ***as long as***, ***provided that***, ***unless*** and ***in case*** are used to show condition. That is, they signal what you can do (the condition) to achieve something. For example: ***If*** *you study very hard, you will do well in your exams. You will not do well in your exams,* ***unless*** *you study very hard.*
- The conjunctions ***so***, ***so ... that*** and ***such ... that*** and connectors ***as a result***, ***therefore***, ***consequently***, ***thus*** and ***hence*** are used to show result. For example: *He drove* ***so*** *fast* ***that*** *he received a speeding fine. The new machines are more productive,* ***thus*** *reducing costs.*

A ***Add the given connector and a clause to complete the following sentences.***

1. You will not go to the movies ______________________________

   ______________________________ (unless)

2. You can go swimming ______________________________

   ______________________________ (as long as)

3. Dress warmly ______________________________

   ______________________________ (in case)

4. Ben can sleep over ______________________________

   ______________________________ (unless)

5. You could become a famous author ______________________________

   ______________________________ (if)

6. You can have your friends over for a party ______________________________

   ______________________________ (provided that)

 ISBN 978-81-8477-750-5

B ***Read Ben's diary entry about his disastrous morning. Underline any conjunctions he uses that show result.***

7th May 2014

Dear Diary,

Today has been such a bad day for me that I have to record it. I hope I can laugh about it later.

I decided to surprise Mum with breakfast in bed. Therefore I got up early and tiptoed downstairs before anyone else had woken up. About half way down, I tripped over my brother's toy truck and landed so heavily that I could hardly breathe. Thus, I lay there for the next few minutes trying to get my breath back.

I didn't want anyone to know about the surprise, so I didn't turn on the light. Consequently, I couldn't see very well. Hence I took out a box of washing powder, instead of pancake mix. As a result, the mixture frothed up all over the kitchen when I tried to beat it. It was an awful mess. Since the pancakes were a failure, I decided on French toast. That was worse. I dropped the bowl on the floor, so I bent to pick up the bread and left the pan on the stove. Therefore the butter caught fire; the smoke alarm started to blare and consequently woke everyone up.

Mum knew that I was only trying to do something special for her and she thanked me. As a result of this morning's escapade, I have decided to keep a torch by my bed.

 ISBN 978-81-8477-750-5

C ***Connect the two sentences using the given conjunctions. You should use commas or semi-colons to separate the clauses.***

1. It was a hot day. Mother packed a picnic and took us to the beach. (since)

2. He was often late. He lost his job. (therefore)

3. Kangaroos feed their young on milk. They are classed as mammals. (hence)

4. He used bright oil paints instead of water-colours. Everyone admired his painting. (because)

5. Mary is not in school today. She has measles. (as)

6. I can't go to school today. I still haven't recovered. (so)

7. James withdrew from the race. His best friend would be sure to win. (so that)

8. It has rained. The farmers can expect good crops this year. (for)

9. A traffic jam holds him up. He will be punctual. (unless)

10. He spoke loudly. Everyone was embarrassed. (so ... that)

 ISBN 978-81-8477-750-5

D ***Contrast connectors** let you compare and contrast information more easily.*

1. Read the following extract from an animal report. Underline the five connectors that indicate the writer is contrasting two pieces of information.

> The shape of a bird's bill can tell a lot about the bird's feeding habits.
>
> Insect-eaters have slender, pointed bills, whereas seed-eaters have short, stout bills for cracking seeds. Fish-eaters, unlike water-strainers who have a spoon-like bill for straining food from the mud, have long sharp bills that they use like a spear. The bill of the mud-prober, however, can be misleading. Although a mud-prober has a long slender bill, it does not use it like a spear. Instead, it probes the mud to chase out small animals.

2. Here are some facts about birds' legs and feet. Use contrast and reason connectors (**however**, **yet**, **whereas**, **instead**, **unlike**, **but**, **although**, **despite**, **so**, **since**) to help you compare the feet of different birds, and say why you think these differences are needed. An example has been done for you.

Perching birds, such as parrots, have toes that lock.	Tree climbers, such as woodpeckers, have wide spread toes with curved claws.	Wading birds, such as flamingoes, have long legs and toes.
Hawks, owls and eagles are birds of prey. They have strong legs and feet with sharp, hooked claws.	Swimming birds, like ducks, puffins and loons, have webbed feet. A grebe swims. It has lobed feet.	Birds known as ground feeders, such as sparrows and domestic hens, have sharp claws with three forward toes and one hind toe.

 ISBN 978-81-8477-750-5

The shape of a bird's feet and the length of its legs provide clues to identify where a bird lives, how it captures its food and how it moves.

1. Perching birds have toes that lock, so they will not fall off the branch when they sleep, but flamingoes have long legs and toes.

2. ______

3. ______

4. ______

5. ______

6. ______

Grammar Help

- ***Connectors*** can be useful, but sometimes they can be tricky. Using too many conjunctions can make your sentences too long and confusing. Good writers vary the length of their sentences.
- Punctuating sentences that have conjunctions can also be tricky. Sometimes you need to use a semi-colon because the pause is longer than a comma and shorter than a full stop. For example: *They had never really liked each other; **now** they were good friends.*

 ISBN 978-81-8477-750-5

E ***Rewrite the passage below to make it less confusing by leaving out some of the underlined connectors. You may have to make other changes too.***

Dan crept silently towards the door of the deserted house and gently eased open the door, then paused before moving into the room so that his eyes could adjust to the dusky interior. The darkness was scary, but somehow comforting because it meant that neither the inhabitants nor anything else could see him; or so he thought, but he was quite wrong.

As Dan tiptoed forward, two pairs of strange yellow eyes followed his steps wherever he went in case he reached the room where his friend, Tom, lay injured and Dan knew that unless he acted swiftly, Tom would not survive because he had fallen a long way; thus not only breaking his leg, but also suffering numerous cuts and scratches.

 ISBN 978-81-8477-750-5

Revision Test

Section 1 (25 marks)

A ***Choose the correct answer for each blank and write its number in the brackets provided.*** (15 marks)

1. A swarm of bees ______________ building a hive outside the house.
   (1) is (2) are
   (3) was (4) were ( )
2. Tom was late for school because he ______________ the school bus and couldn't hail a cab.
   (1) miss (2) was missing
   (3) could miss (4) had missed ( )
3. This fantastic book is ______________ than the one you are reading.
   (1) most exciting (2) less exciting
   (3) more exciting (4) exciting ( )
4. I'm not sure to ______________ I should give this entry form.
   (1) whom (2) which
   (3) who (4) that ( )
5. A police officer wears ______________ navy blue uniform.
   (1) an (2) the
   (3) a (4) his ( )
6. I don't have ______________ milk on my cereal.
   (1) many (2) much
   (3) some (4) a little ( )
7. ______________ you work faster, we will not finish before dark.
   (1) If (2) Unless
   (3) Since (4) Because ( )

 ISBN 978-81-8477-750-5

8. There is finally peace ______________ the two warring tribes.

(1) with (2) among

(3) for (4) between ( )

9. I ______________ you many times and you still have not visited me.

(1) am inviting (2) invited

(3) have invited (4) had invited ( )

10. I prefer watching movies at the theatre ______________ watching movies on television.

(1) with (2) to

(3) than (4) by ( )

11. You ______________ believe everything you hear.

(1) must (2) would

(3) ought to (4) shouldn't ( )

12. My mum and dad always ______________ each other.

(1) agree with (2) agree on

(3) agree to (4) agree about ( )

13. If I invite you to my party, you will come, ______________ you?

(1) will (2) would

(3) won't (4) wouldn't ( )

14. ______________ the twins ______________ May knows where Mrs Jones lives.

(1) Either ... and (2) Not ... nor

(3) Neither ... nor (4) Not ... but also ( )

15. My sister, who is playing tonight, ______________ the violin since she was three.

(1) learned (2) has been learning

(3) has learned (4) is learning ( )

 ISBN 978-81-8477-750-5

B ***Complete each sentence with the correct word or words from the brackets.*** (10 marks)

16. I had to go to the doctor because I was suffering ______________ (with, from, by) a high fever.

17. Venus is the ______________ (most close, closer, closest) planet to Earth.

18. The kind ______________ (witch's, witches', witches's) broomstick lay on the bed next to her pointed hat.

19. Neither Tom nor the girls ______________ (are, is, was) at the library today.

20. Although they ______________ (could, used to, will) be best friends, Jane and Sally seldom see each other now that they are older.

21. The little boy walked as ______________ (quick, quicker, quickly) as he could to keep up with his mother.

22. The tap will continue to drip ______________ (unless, since, because) you put a new washer in it.

23. The students ______________ (are waiting, have waited, will wait) since 2:00 pm for the Mayor to arrive.

24. The opposing teams ______________ (put aside, put off, put forward) their rivalry and celebrated together.

25. The hunter reluctantly drew out his rifle as the pride of lions ______________ (have, has, had) never before approached so close to the camp.

 ISBN 978-81-8477-750-5

Section 2 (25 marks)
Cloze Passages

C ***Fill in each blank with the correct word from the box. There will be three words left over at the end of the exercise.*** (15 marks)

on	**with**	**my**	**while**	**when**	**would**
off	**will**	**but**	**between**	**they**	**whose**
of	**might**	**the**	**among**	**won't**	**can**

I have never been mountain trekking before, (26) ______________ I would love to try it. My friend David, (27) ______________ parents love to trek, often take him (28) ______________ them when they go. He said that I (29) ______________ be able to join them (30) ______________ they go next week. It must be very peaceful walking (31) ______________ the many pine trees that grow (32) ______________ the mountain slopes.

On long walks, David sometimes paddles in a mountain stream (33) ______________ his parents take a rest. He takes (34) ______________ his boots and rolls up his jeans so that they (35) ______________ get wet. I know that I (36) ______________ appreciate the wildflowers that grow on (37) ______________ slopes. If there are any deer in the woods, I (38) ______________ photograph them, as my uncle gave me a camera for (39) ______________ birthday. I hope (40) ______________ ask me to go with them next week.

 ISBN 978-81-8477-750-5

D ***Fill in each blank with the correct word from the box. There will be five words left over when you have completed the exercise.*** (10 marks)

consequently	**seldom**	**unless**	**else**	**therefore**
although	**usually**	**but**	**if**	**because**
whenever	**however**	**either**	**when**	**sometimes**

I don't know why, but (41) ______________ I travel by public transport, the buses are always crowded and (42) ______________ I have to stand up on the way to work. It may be better (43) ______________ I were to leave home earlier. As it is, many passengers are left behind, (44) ______________ they force those standing to move further down the aisle. I (45) ______________ have to wait for up to twenty minutes for another bus (46) ______________ the one that arrives is full up. (47) ______________, I have been late to work a few times. My manager is (48) ______________ sympathetic. I don't think it will be long (49) ______________, before he begins to lose his patience. Perhaps I should buy (50) ______________ a motorbike or a small car.

Section 1:	**/25**
Section 2:	**/25**
TOTAL	**/50**

 ISBN 978-81-8477-750-5

Page 1

A 1. gratitude 2. kindness 3. hope
4. relief 5. despair 6. joy

Page 2

B *Possible answers*:
1. tell the truth 2. in danger
3. for their wickedness
4. their hatred 5. for their beauty

C 2. **-ment**: enjoyment, agreement, punishment
3. **-y**: discovery, honesty, injury
4. **-ion**: creation, action, introduction

Page 3

D 1. multiplication 2. division
3. explanation 4. instruction
5. laziness 6. approval
7. corrections 8. confidence
9. solution

E *Possible answers*
1. band of musicians, troupe of actors/ singers
2. congregation of churchgoers/ worshippers, choir of singers
3. bench of judges
4. horde of natives, tribe of natives/ monkeys, pride of lions
5. string of pearls, pair of earrings, set of diamonds
6. pod of whales, school of fish, shoal of herring
7. comb of bananas, set of plates

Page 4

F 1. was 2. does 3. is 4. are
5. is 6. are 7. are 8. is
9. is 10. rushes

Page 5

A 1. you 2. you 3. you 4. I
5. we 6. us 7. myself 8. I
9. me 10. myself

Page 6

B 2. possessive pron
3. indefinite pron
4. demonstrative pron
5. possessive pron
6. indefinite pron
7. personal pron
8. reciprocal pron
9. personal pron
10. demonstrative pron, possessive pron

Page 7

C *Answers may vary.*

Page 8

D 2. yours, possessive pronoun
3. someone, indefinite pronoun
4. each other, reciprocal pronoun
5. that, demonstrative pronoun
6. they/you, personal pronoun (subject)
7. mine, possessive pronoun
8. these, demonstrative pronoun
9. They, personal pronoun (subject)
10. me, personal pronoun (object)

Page 9

A 1. himself 2. yourself
3. itself 4. myself
5. herself 6. himself
7. themselves 8. themselves
9. herself 10. themselves
11. itself 12. itself/themselves

Page 10

B 1. ourselves 2. yourself
3. myself 4. themselves
5. herself 6. himself
7. itself 8.. yourselves

Page 11

C 2. Whose torn trousers are over there?
3. What has made those marks on the floor?
4. Who is the girl sitting over there?
5. What do you want to study when you go to university?
6. Which is your favourite film?
7. Whom does your father support in the English Premier League?

Page 12

D 1. whom 2. who 3. Who
4. who 5. whom 6. who
7. who 8. whom

Page 13

A 1. who 2. which/that
3. who 4. which/that, which/ that
5. who 6. whom
7. whose 8. which / that
9. which/that
10. which/ that, which / that
11. who, which/that
12. whose

Page 14

B 1. whose hands were covered in flour
2. whose shirt was torn
3. whose parents were very rich
4. whose mother often works late
5. whose father often buys her books
6. whose face was recognized by witnesses
7. whose book won a national award
8. whose branches were thick and leafy
9. whose father is a good pianist
10. whose sister is in our netball team

Page 15

C *Answers may vary.*

Page 16

D *Answers may vary.*

Page 17

A *Answers may vary.* B *Answers may vary.*

Page 19

C **Size:** narrow, thick, tall, short
Quality: cruel, foolish, dangerous, irate
Origin: Japanese, English, Singaporean, Scottish
Classification: wooden, plastic, shopping, public

Page 20

D 1. The huge, old lion crouched in the long, dry, yellow grass.
2. Nothing tastes better than warm, buttery, homemade chocolate biscuits.
3. The tiny, inquisitive, black cat sniffed around the giant oak tree.
4. Mrs Brown gave John a useful, new, black, Japanese calculator.
5. The small, ancient, wooden boat tossed about on the vast, angry sea.
6. Mrs Taylor placed the elegant, antique French clock on the brown, wooden table.

Page 21

E 1. smiling 2. mountainous
3. medical 4. useless
5. rusty 6. tropica
I 7. boiled 8. selfish
9. sorrowful 10. memorable

Page 22

F 1. (a) expensive (b) scenic
(c) comfortable, comforting
(d) friendly (e) wooden, woody
(f) caring
(g) poisonous, poisoned
(h) stormy, storming
(i) foolish (j) bored, boring
2. *Adjectives used in crossword:* expensive, scenic, comfortable, friendly, woody, poisoned, stormy, foolish, bored
3. (a) selfish (b) free
(c) red (d) helpful

Page 24

A 1. *Adjectives of quantity* (circled): one, two, three, some, several, eight
Ordinary adjectives (underlined): lonely, squawking, long-haired, happy, tiny, graceful

Page 25

B 1. thirteen 2. fifty-two 3. eight
4. five 5. twelve 6. ninety

Page 25

C *Suggested answers*:
2. The long/grey gown is the more elegant.
3. The fur overcoat is the longest.
4. The floral sundress is less expensive.
5. The pair of sandals is the least expensive.
6. The raincoat is the plainest.
7. The joggers/sandals are the most comfortable.

Page 27

D *Possible answers include:*
Tom King is the oldest of the three writers.
Sam Prince is the youngest of the three writers.
Jim Lord is older than Sam Prince (but younger than Tom King).
Jim Lord's comics sell better than the other two.
Tom King is the most athletic/ musical.
Sam Prince is the least athletic /mobile of the writers.
Sam Prince writes the funniest stories.
Tom King writes the most serious stories.
Jim Lord's books are the most violent.

Page 28

E *Possible answers*:
3. Parachuting is the most dangerous of the three activities.
4. Exercising is more important for your health than brushing your hair or cleaning your teeth.
5. I feel more nervous about meeting a savage dog than going to the dentist.
6. Pianists are the most skilful of the three.
7. Books about explorers are more interesting than the other two types.
8. A bicycle is more expensive than a skipping rope.

Page 29

F 1. good, better, best
2. worst, bad, worse
3. farther/further, far, farthest/furthest
4. many, more, most
5. little, least, less
6. elder, old, eldest

Page 31

A slowly, silently, carelessly, briefly, painfully, slowly, surely. (*NOTE*: 'nearly' is an adverb of degree, not manner.)

Page 32

B 1. (a) sobbed hysterically
(b) repeated endlessly
(c) boasted proudly
(d) moaned painfully
(e) enquired curiously
(f) stammered nervously
(g) warned helpfully

Page 33

2. *Answers may vary.*

Page 34

C *Answers may vary.*

Page 35

D through James' hard work, with the help of his friends, by their actions, with utmost respect, by train, on foot, by bus, on bicycles, without funding, without recognition, through personal sacrifice

 ISBN 978-81-8477-750-5

Page 36
E *Answers may vary.*

Page 38
A 1. hard 2. nervous
3. steadily 4. confident
5. beautiful 6. well
7. tired 8. expressive
9. highly 10. talented

Page 39
B really (Adv), totally (V), entirely (V), quite (Adj), extremely (Adj), so (Adv), exceptionally (Adj), completely (V), absolutely (V), just (Adj)

Page 40
C *Answers may vary.*

Page 41
D *Answers may vary.*

Page 43
A *Answers may vary.*

Page 44
B *Answers may vary.*

Page 45
C 1. present participles 2. gerunds
3. adjectives 4. gerunds
5. present participles 6. adjectives
7. present participles 8. gerunds

Page 46
D 1. waiting 2. sailing 3. skating
4. walking 5. painting 6. shopping
7. exercising 8. scrubbing 9. reading

Page 47
E 2. No cycling 3. No parking
4. No diving 5. No fishing
6. No littering 7. No crossing
8. No swimming 9. No camping

Page 48
A 1. at 2. for 3. by 4. along 5. until
6. at 7. On 8. by 9. to 10. from
11. to 12. on 13. After 14. for

Page 49
B 2. return 3. employ 4. extinguish
5. phone 6. delay 7. suggest
8. refuse 9. cancel 10. deliver
11. start

Page 50
C 2. Def. (a) 3. Def (b) 4. Def (c)
5. Def(a) 6. Def (d) 7. Def (c)
8. Def (b)

Page 51
D 1. asked out 2. asked for
3. asked in 4. closing down
5. closing in 6. cut up
7. cut down 8. cut off
9. cut out
10. set in, set off, set up, set out
11. put down, put ... away, put off, put back

Page 52
A *Suggested answers*:
2. You should report to the Reception when you arrive at the hospital.
3. You should sign your cheque before going to the bank teller. (This saves time.)
4. You should go to the waiting lounge at Gate 5 when you are on transit at the airport.
5. You should keep your dog a leash at the park. (It makes it safer for everyone.)
6. You should not leave valuable items in your room at the hotel. (You should put them in the safety deposit box at the Reception desk.)
7. You should take care of your wallet at the shopping centre. (You need to look out for pickpockets.)
8. You should not feed the monkeys at the zoo. (They need to eat special food.)

Page 54
B *Answers may vary.*
C *Possible answers*:
1. I could put the wrapper in a bin.
2. I/We might go to Malaysia.
3. The coach would substitute someone else for me.
4. I might make a snowman.
5. I could get a vase for my Mum.
6. You could show me some other models. *(Notice the change in the modal)*

Page 55
D *Suggested answers*:
2. You would get a hot, cross bunny.
3. They might eat fish and ships.
4. You should give him a hand.
5. You would get a dingbat.
6. He might keep it in a snowbank.
7. You could eat it on Saturday.
8. He must give up treating people when he runs out of patience.

Page 56
E *Answers may vary.*

Page 58
A *Possible answers include*:
2. people order, waiters serve, chef cooks
3. cows moo, sheep bleat, tractor ploughs, workers harvest
4. children swim, people sunbathe, wind blows
5. spectators cheer, players kick, goalkeeper saves/dives
6. people read/ look for books/check the catalogue
7. shoppers buy / choose/ bargain, stallholders sell/ chat
8. athletes run / jump, starter shoots gun, scorers tally

Page 59
B I <u>clamber</u> **(clambered)** like a bear up the...
Into the leafy crown I <u>creep</u> **(crept)**, ...
Across rough branches that <u>scrape</u> **(scraped)** my knees
Over twigs that <u>prick</u> **(pricked)** and <u>prod</u> **(prodded)**
Until I <u>reach</u> **(reached)** the safety of my ...
That <u>sways</u> **(swayed)** and <u>bends</u> **(bent)** to the will of the wind
And <u>becomes</u> **(became)** a pirate ship ...
Here I <u>stay</u> **(stayed)** wrapped in dreams until Mother <u>calls</u> **(called)**, ...

Page 60
C *Answer may vary.*

Page 61
D 1. lived, found, called, worked, slaved, owned, drank, dressed, ate, paid, could, wore, farmed, sold, lived, made, had, protected, helped, travelled, moved, arrived, held. *NOTE: These are not simple past tense*: made of, was ... sung, (was) told, was provided
2. *Possible answers*
(b) I live a hard life. I pay high taxes. I wear ... I live in .... (etc)
(c) I travel from town to town, I pass on the news. I sing my news.
(d) I drink fine wine, I dress in delicate silks. I eat off silver platters.

Page 62
A *Possible answers*:
2. I think the girl is trying to score a goal / shoot a basket.
3. I think the man is reading a book.
4. I think the boy is brushing his teeth.
5. I think the old lady is climbing (up) a ladder.
6. I think the man is rocking a baby (to sleep).
7. I think the old man is driving a car.
8. I think the woman is riding on a bus / standing in a bus.

Page 63
B *Answers may vary.*
C 1. am trying 2. is rattling 3. is yowling
4. are blaring 5. are yelling 6. am tossing
7. am praying 8. are sleeping

Page 64
D 2. The dog is burying a bone.
3. (the gardener) is planting a tree.
4. (the miner) is looking for gold.
5. It is going/starting to rain.
6. (the athletes) are competing in a race.
7. The bull is chasing the boy.
8. She is catching a bus.
9. They are watching a clown.
10. He is telling jokes.
11. He is playing a trick.
12. She is getting tickled.

Page 65
E *Possible answers:*
1. is cooking dinner at present
2. is just taking a bath
3. is still talking on the phone to his girlfriend
4. are talking to me now

Page 66
A *Suggested answers*:
2. The netball team has won a trophy.
3. Dad has (just) washed his car.
4. Ben has (just) missed the train.
5. Sue has weeded the flowerbed.
6. Spot has eaten all the chocolate.
7. Bob has been jogging. /Bob has lost weight jogging.
8. The painting has fallen off the wall.
9. Someone has stolen Madam Lim's ruby necklace.

Page 68
B 1. My sister has always played tennis on Sundays.
2. My parents have not eaten at the new restaurant yet.
3. A few students have not tried their best to excel this year.
4. The music students have just arrived in the hall with their instruments.
5. My favourite aunt has not visited us since last August.
6. Jane has not lived in Australia for very long.
7. Sam, a keen reader, has already read all the books in the class library.
8. The train has already left the station.
9. My old uncle has never needed reading glasses to read his paper.

Page 69
C *Answers may vary.*

Page 70
D *Possible answers:*
3. She has not yet fed the cat./She still has not fed the cat.
4. She has just/already swept the floor.
5. She has already/just turned out the cupboard.
6. She has not cut the vegetables yet./She still has not cut the vegetables.
7. She has already/just drunk up the milk.
8. She has not bought the bread yet./She still has not bought the bread.

Page 72
A 2. (They) were playing chess when the phone rang.
3. (Mark) was putting on his shoes when the phone rang.
4. (He) was going to bed when the phone rang.

 ISBN 978-81-8477-750-5

5. (Dad) was cooking in the kitchen when the electricity failed.
6. (He) was working at the computer when the electricity failed.
7. (He) was walking down the stairs when the electricity failed.

Page 73

B *Possible answers:*
1. Last Sunday, they were picnicking at the beach when it started to rain.
2. Last evening, we were hailing/waiting for a taxi when it started to rain.
3. Half an hour ago, we were walking in the park when it started to rain.

Page 74

C 1. were doing 2. were working
3. were digging 4. were gardening
5. were planting 6. was playing
7. was taking 8. was putting
9. was helping 10. was watching
11. was shopping 12. was keeping
13. was wearing

Page 75

D 1. was walking 2. was wearing
3. was shining 4. was squinting
5. walked 6. were moving
7. were waiting 8. saw
9. turned 10. hit
11. was lying 12. was trembling
13. touched 14. was glaring

Page 76

E *Possible answers:*
2. On Tuesday, when Suzanne was smelling a flower, a bee stung her.
3. On Wednesday, as she was cycling with friends, the tyre burst.
4. On Thursday, while she was showing off her skating, she crashed into a dustbin.
5. On Friday, when she was crying over her lost dog, her favourite star walked by.

Page 77

A had become, had enrolled, had travelled, had arrived, had transferred, had been forced, had been, had caught, had played

Page 78

B 1. had planted 2. had started 3. had left
4. had eaten 5. had shown 6. had tried
7. had called 8. had swum

C *Suggested answers:*
2. After Bob had observed the exhaust emission, he turned off the engine.
3. After Bob had drained off the oil, he did not check the spark plugs.
4. After Bob had filled in new oil, he did not top up the radiator.
5. After Bob had started the car again, he tuned the engine.
6. After Bob had shaken out the mats, he vacuumed the inside of the car.

Page 79

D *Answers may vary.*

Page 80

E 2. June told me that her sister had caught chicken pox.
3. Mary asked me what had happened to change my mind.
4. Jill demanded to know who had taken her ruler.
5. Miss Lee reminded us that we had left a mess in the art room.
6. He explained that he had been suffering from the flu.
7. Mr Pereira warned me that he had had enough of my nonsense.
8. John said that he had already seen that movie.
9. Sue yelled excitedly that the post had arrived.

Page 81

F *Suggested answers:*
2. A dog had chased them there.
3. Someone had asked them to deliver a parcel.
4. It had rained and they had wanted to shelter from the rain.
5. The old man had fallen off the ladder and they had gone to help him.
6. The wind had blown their umbrella away, and it had snagged itself in the tree.
7. The pile of leaves had caught fire and they had come to put out the flames.

Page 82

A Mr Ross: I'm about to leave, will be visiting.
Ms Lee: I'll come
Mr Ross: I'm attending, who'll be, I'm going to take, It's
Ms Lee: are going to be, Shall
Mr Ross: I'm about to sign, shall
Ms Lee: are you doing
Mr Ross: I'm entertaining, arrives, plan
Ms Lee: are not going to wait,They'll cancel
Mr Ross: I'll see, I'll see

Page 83

B *Answers may vary.*

Page 84

C *Possible answers:*
2. I'm visiting Grandma with the family.
3. We're taking Grandma out for lunch.
4. I'm going for Sally's birthday party.
5. I'm meeting Tom to return some books I borrowed.
6. I'm having an early dinner.
7. I'm baby-sitting for the Lees until 10.00 pm.

Page 85

D is making, (is) filling /are standing, are feeling / is wearing, is clutching / is panting / are crying, is standing, is carrying
3. The holidays are about to begin.
4. The Brown family are about to go fishing.
5. The boys are about to see the Principal.
6. They are about to be scolded.
7. Janet is about to go to work.
8. The basketball final is about to end.
9. John is about to shoot a goal.
10. Kim and Robert are about to be married.

Page 87

A 1. plays — <u>the trombone</u>
2. wants — <u>a new car</u> 3. wrote — <u>a report</u>
4. don't want — <u>to borrow this book</u>.
5. visits — <u>her grandmother</u>.
6. chased — <u>the thief</u>. 7. is knitting — <u>a scarf</u>
8. are building — <u>a nest</u>

Page 88

B *Verbs (not all have objects)*: wrote, worked is considered, shared, attended, learnt, apprenticed, started, tricked, wrote, printed, began, invented, discovered, taught set up, went on
Direct objects: books, diplomat, one of American history's most famous statesmen, his childhood, school, his father's trade, himself, to write articles, his brother, his own newspaper, experimenting with electricity, the lightning rod, two kinds of electricity, many foreign languages, a college, to become one of the greatest statesmen America has ever known

C *Answers may vary.*

Page 89

D 1. Mother buys (Grandma) <u>flowers</u>.
2. The waitress brought (us) <u>the menu</u>.
3. The company gave (Sam) <u>a gold watch</u>.
4. Mother showed (Daisy) <u>the broken cup</u> ...
5. Dan is catching his (sister) <u>a butterfly</u>.

Page 90

E *Suggested answers:*
1. Mother is feeding baby some cereal.
2. Father is glancing at the newspaper.
3. Grandma has knitted herself a shawl.
4. Ben is giving the dog some food.
5. Grandpa is writing Mark a letter.
6. The cat is scratching the mat.
7. Aunt Susan has baked baby a cake.
8. May is drawing a picture for her mother.

Page 91

A *Transitive verbs* (circled): lifted, struck, flexed, raised, smashed, wanted, handed, wiped, studied, was, threw, would collect
Intransitive verbs: descended, bent, paused, drank, grunted
Objects(underlined): the heavy hammer, the anvil, his muscles, the hammer, the iron bar, the shape a glass of ale ("his master" is the indirect verb), his mouth, the horseshoe he was making, a fine shoe, the horseshoe, his money

Page 92

B 1. <u>echoed</u> ✗ 2. <u>took off</u> ✓
3. <u>drove</u> ✓ 4. <u>arrived</u> ✗
5. <u>contained</u> ✓ 6. <u>were hung</u> ✗
7. <u>broke</u> ✓ 8. <u>nominated</u> ✓
9. <u>read</u> ✗ 10. <u>stayed</u> ✗

C 1. a carriage 2. eyesight 3. houses & offices
4. stamps 5. animals 6. medicine
7. ancient human artifacts
8. dead animals for display

Page 93

D 1. The plane took off very late. I
He took off his coat and tie. T
2. Someone broke into the house. T
A tramp broke in and made a mess. I
3. John turned on the light. T
The canoe turned over in the rapids. I
4. She stood out in a crowd. I
John stood for elections. T
5. We got away after an hour. I
The thief got away with the jewels. T
6. The injection will wear off soon. I
Don't wear out my patience. T
7. Hang onto the rope or you'll fall. T
Please volunteer—don't hang back. I
8. Look out! That car is speeding! I
Help me look for a phone, please. T

E 1. lay, lay (T) 2. are lying (I)
3. are laying (T) 4. Lie (I)
5. lay (I) 6. has ... laid (T)
7. has ... lain (I) 8. laid (T)

Page 94

F *Answers may vary.*

Page 95

A 1. <u>because</u> it was her birthday.
2. <u>as</u> it was too late to post invitations.
3. <u>since</u> his cousin was coming to stay.
4. <u>as</u> she wanted to invite his cousin also.
5. <u>in case</u> her friends had made other plans.
6. <u>for</u> all the arrangements she had to make.
7. <u>so</u> she could organize everything.
8. <u>because</u> she had planned well.

Page 96

B *Answers may vary.*

Page 97

C 1. we plan to drive to Malacca.
2. the brakes would be reliable.

 ISBN 978-81-8477-750-5

3. store some food for the journey.
4. it rains.
5. we can find a cheap motel.
6. be ready well before we leave.
7. be ready for any emergencies.

Page 98

D 1. Since she did not want to upset her mother, ... Reason
2. As long as his father was in hospital, ... Condition
3. Because she had homework, ... Reason
4. In order to complete his homework, ... Purpose
5. Unless her mother allowed, ... Condition
6. As John couldn't dance, ... Reason
7. If she could leave early, ... Condition
8. In case his father needed him, ... Reason & Purpose

Page 99

E *Suggested answers*:
1. tried to coax the kitten down with some milk.
2. tried to climb up the tree
3. climbing, she fell out of the tree.
4. standing on a box to reach the kitten.
5. she carried out a ladder, but it was too short.
6. Susan ran out of ideas, she asked her father what to do.
7. called the fire brigade for help.
8. a fireman rescued the kitten.
9. the kitten was safely in Susan's arms, she thanked the fireman.

Page 100

A *Answers may vary.*

Page 101

B such ... that (*para 1*) / Therefore, so ... that, Thus (*para 2*) / so, Consequently, Hence, As a result, since, so, Therefore, consequently (*para 3*) /
As a result (*para 4*)

Page 102

C 1. Since it was a hot day, Mother packed a picnic and took us to the beach.
2. He was often late; therefore he lost his job.
3. Kangaroos feed their young on milk; hence they are classed as mammals.
4. Because he used bright oil paints instead of water-colours, everyone admired his painting. / Everyone admired his painting because he used bright oil paints instead of water-colours.
5. Mary is not in school today as she has measles.
6. I still haven't recovered, so I can't go to school today.
7. James withdrew from the race so that his best friend would be sure to win.
8. The farmers can expect good crops this year, for it has rained.
9. He will be punctual unless a traffic jam holds him up. / Unless a traffic jam holds him up, he will be punctual.
10. He spoke so loudly that everyone was embarrassed.

Page 103

D 1. whereas, unlike, however, although, instead
2. *Answers may vary.*

Page 105

E *Suggested answers*:
Dan crept silently towards the door of the deserted house and gently eased open the door. He paused before moving into the room so that his eyes could adjust to the dusky interior. The darkness was scary, but somehow comforting; it meant that neither the inhabitants nor anything else could see him; or so he thought. He was quite wrong. As Dan tiptoed forward, two pairs of strange yellow eyes followed his steps wherever he went. He reached the room where his friend, Tom, lay injured. Dan knew that unless he acted swiftly, Tom would not survive because he had fallen a long way, suffering numerous cuts and scratches.

Pages 106–110: Revision Test

A 1. (1) 2. (4) 3. (3) 4. (1)
5. (3) 6. (2) 7. (2) 8. (4)
9. (3) 10. (2) 11. (4) 12. (1)
13. (3) 14. (3) 15. (2)

B 16. from 17. closest
18. witch's 19. are
20. used to 21. quickly
22. unless 23. have waited
24. put aside 25. had

C 26. but 27. whose
28. with 29. might
30. when 31. among
32. on 33. while
34. off 35. won't
36. will 37. the
38. can 39. my
40. they

D 41. whenever 42. therefore
43. if 44. unless
45. sometimes 46. because
47. Consequently 48. usually
49. however 50. either

 ISBN 978-81-8477-750-5